LEARNING RESOURCES CTR/NEW ENGLAND TECH.
GEN   HD5854.N94 1988
Nye, David,   Alternative staffing strat

3 0147 0001 3471 1

HD5854 .N94

Nye, David, 1941-

Alternative staffing strategies

W9-CZB-766

DATE DUE

JUL 0 5 1993		
OCT 27 1994		

DEMCO 38-297

Alternative Staffing Strategies

Alternative Staffing Strategies

David Nye

The Bureau of National Affairs, Inc., Washington, D.C.

Copyright © 1988
The Bureau of National Affairs, Inc.

Library of Congress Cataloging-in-Publication Data

Nye, David, 1941–
    Alternative staffing strategies.

    Bibliography: p.
    Includes index.
    I. Employees, Temporary.   2. Temporary employment.
I. Title.
HD5854.N94   1988   658.3′01   87-35857
ISBN 0-87179-548-5

Authorization to photocopy items for internal or personal use, or the internal
or personal use of specific clients, is granted by BNA Books for libraries
and other users registered with the Copyright Clearance Center (CCC)
Transactional Reporting Service, provided that $0.50 per page is paid di-
rectly to CCC, 21 Congress St., Salem, MA 01970, 0-87179-548-5/88/$0 +
.50

Printed in the United States of America
International Standard Book Number 0-87179-548-5

This book is dedicated to the memory of my father, Willard L. Nye; and to my magic wife and sons: Judy, Jimmy, Andy, and Rick; and to Mom.

Preface

*Sergeant, don't ever involve me in another personnel matter—
the entire area's a quagmire.*

> (Lieutenant Buntz to Sergeant Yablonski,
> from an episode of *Hill Street Blues*)

It is often said that change is the only constant. Few grasp
that truth more readily than practitioners of the art and science of
management. The employment strategies that are the subject of
this book are at once outgrowths of and management responses to
unprecedented changes in American social and economic priorities.
The book was written for the people who must cope with those
changes as they affect the roles of individuals in organizations—
human resource managers, line managers, and business owners in
the private sector, as well as government managers with staffing
authority. The book has two main purposes: to identify these new
options for human resources deployment; and to provide criteria
by which readers may evaluate the potential value of those options
to their organizations.

Except for a special report prepared by The Bureau of National
Affairs, Inc., in 1986 and brief accounts in the popular press, little
has been written about contemporary alternative employment
strategies. The formal studies reported in scholarly journals and
government publications tend to focus on single strategies, and it
is difficult to compare their results due to differences in time frames
and terminology. For example, there is no standard definition of
"older worker" or "leased employee." This book attempts to bring
together discussions of several key human resource strategies so
that they may be compared more readily; it also strives to identify,
and thus minimize the effect of, the related semantic problems.

The five alternative employment strategies explored here are
not mutually exclusive; they may be used in combination with each

other and with traditional employment arrangements. Nor are they all-inclusive; there are other ways work can be done in organizations outside the usual employer-employee compact. The approaches discussed in this book were selected because they seem to hold the most promise for the greatest number of organizations.

Because of differences in the novelty and complexity of employment strategies, there is some variation in the organization of the chapters. In general, however, each chapter begins by giving an operational definition of the employment mode that is its subject and a brief summary of its current use. Case studies then show how specific organizations are integrating the employment mode with their overall strategic and tactical business plans. The advantages and disadvantages of each approach are analyzed from a management perspective, and specific recommendations are made for addressing them in management decision making and for implementing them.

Throughout the book, the views of management attorneys, consultants, industry spokespersons, academicians, and representatives of government agencies that regulate employment matters have been incorporated. In addition to drawing on many secondary sources, the author personally interviewed some 30 individuals involved in the planning, implementation, and oversight of alternative employment strategies. Direct quotations and attributed statements not cited in the end-of-chapter notes are taken from those interviews.

The author is grateful to the following people, who contributed their time and expertise to the preparation of this manuscript: Carmen Arno, Arno and Associates; Robert Becker, Mt. Prospect Lawnmower Company; Wendy Black, Best Western International, Inc.; J. Andrew Butler, Staff Services, Inc.; Keith Crossland, Consolidated Employee Benefits Corporation; Jerome Dreyer, Association of Data Processing Service Organizations; Jack Durkin, Stouffer Foods Corp.; Charles DeBow, Motorola Semiconductor Product Sector; David Gamse, American Association of Retired Persons; Susan Glaser, Comprehensive Rehabilitation Services, Inc.; Robert Gentry, The Browning Group; Gil Gordon, Gil Gordon Associates; Addie Johnson, Bank of America; Rick Higgins, Pacific Bell; Carl Kirkpatrick, J.C. Penney Co.; Edward Kovacic, Motorola Inc.; Ronald James, Squire, Sanders & Dempsey; Jules Lichtenstein, Small Business Administration; Cathy Lewis, Resource: Careers; Lisa Martinez, Manpower Temporary Services; Alice McCray, A.F. McCray Consulting Services; Cheryl Parker, Vista Chemical

Company; Thomas Plewes, Bureau of Labor Statistics; Diane Rothberg, Association of Part-Time Professionals; Sam Saaco, National Association of Temporary Services; J. Marshall Seelander, National Technical Services Association; Marvin Selter, National Staff Leasing Association; Marjorie Shorrock, Resource: Careers; Joy Simonson, U.S. House of Representatives; Michael Solomon, Hahn, Loeser & Parks; Ronald White, National Employer, Inc.; and Leslie Young, ATAC.

The author thanks Camille Christie, Timothy Darby, Mary Green Miner, and Francis Hill Slowinski of BNA Books, whose thoughtful guidance contributed greatly in the preparation of this book.

Contents

1

Introduction

What Are Alternative Staffing Strategies?

Perhaps the best way to define "alternative staffing strategies" is first to define what they are alternatives *to*: the traditional employer-employee relationship. In general, this relationship is characterized by a worker's being hired into what is loosely termed a "permanent" association with the employer. While an employment agency or executive search firm may bring the parties together, there is no continuing involvement of a third party (save for collective bargaining representatives). Except for fixed holidays and vacations, the employee works year-around at the employer's place of business. It is assumed that, unless the employee resigns or is fired, he or she will remain with the employer until death or retirement. In addition to cash compensation, the employee receives benefits designed at least in part to reward and encourage continued service. If a downturn in business requires an employee furlough, the employer maintains the relationship through both legally required and voluntary payments and other forms of support. Examples include severance pay, unemployment insurance, continuation of service credits for employee benefits purposes, recall policies, and other actions based on the expectation that the employee will return to active service. The parties have the legal rights and responsibilities accorded them by both common law and a myriad of statutes and regulations governing the employer-employee relationship.

Alternative staffing strategies, then, represent methods through which an employer offers work, and workers perform it, in a way that departs from these elements of the traditional approach.

1

The Modern Evolution of Alternative Strategies

There is nothing new about alternative employment arrangements. For example, temporary help service firms have been active in the U.S. employment market since the end of World War II. Companies have leased truck drivers and security forces for decades. In 1975, Gannon observed that the number of "peripheral" workers was increasing rapidly, correctly noting that the trend was then "a fact not generally recognized."[1] That overall growth has continued. Today, an even greater proportion of the work force is employed under alternative staffing schemes. Many of these individuals perform tasks requiring high levels of skill and professional training. There is a high probability that these arrangements will become commonplace in the U.S. labor market.

While traditional relationships will remain the norm, this book illustrates why alternative arrangements cannot be viewed merely as responses to transient labor-market problems. In general, the increasing popularity of nontraditional work relationships can be explained in terms of changes in both employer and employee perspectives.

Employer Perspectives

The term *strategy*, as it applies to alternative employment arrangements, is useful here. It generally refers to broad plans designed to accomplish top management's long-range mission. Faced with aggressive global competition and the threat of hostile corporate takeovers, however, few modern corporations can afford to dwell on such vagaries as "mission." As summarized by *The New York Times*,

> Survival must now be the chief executive's overriding concern. The new order eschews loyalty to workers, products, corporate structure, businesses, factories, communities, even the nation. All such allegiances are viewed as expendable under the new rules. With survival at stake, only market leadership, strong profits and a high stock price can be allowed to matter.

The *Times* quoted David T. Kearns, chairman of Xerox Corporation: "Most of us who are running major companies may not understand yet how much we will have to do differently to be successful." After years of manufacturing copiers only in America, Xerox now imports parts and machines and has laid off half its American factory workers.[2]

Thus, if the corporate mission is literal, short-run survival, the concomitant human-resource strategies are cost effectiveness and flexibility. Many alternative staffing arrangements offer both, hence their link to corporate strategy.

At the same time that corporate and public-sector top managements are slashing their work forces, they express concern about the morale and productivity of the survivors. The *Times* noted that "executives face the difficult paradox of having to convince employees that they really care about them—until the axe falls in the next wave of cutbacks."[3] As will be seen later in this book, employers in both the public and private sectors have used contract employees as a way out of this dilemma, employing them as a buffer to insulate a core work force of regular employees from reductions in force.

Finally, changing technology is also prompting companies to experiment with alternative staffing plans. In some cases—most notably that of "telecommuting"—the technology is related to the work itself. In other cases, computer technology allows employers to maintain data on and handle personnel administration of large pools of "on-call" workers who move in and out of the work force with some frequency. Similar technology allows third-party suppliers, such as employee leasing and temporary help service firms, to match workers to very specific employer needs and to train employees to high skill levels in such areas as word processor and personal computer operation.

Employee Perspectives

In 1985, an average 18 million workers—one out of six—was working part time. In one month of that year, nearly 9 million workers spent at least eight hours a week working at home. Between 1970 and 1986, the number of people employed by temporary help firms grew from 184,000 to 760,000. Overall, there are an estimated 28 million "contingent workers," including part-time and temporary employees, the self-employed, and persons working for firms supplying computer and guard services.[4] Some of these individuals would prefer permanent, full-time work, but this has always been so. Alternative staffing arrangements are more prevalent today in part because they satisfy *wants* as well as needs. William A. Schiemann, vice-president of Opinion Research Corporation, has noted that beyond such factors as child-care responsibilities, "lifestyles have also changed. Individuals value more time away from work."[5]

Among both young and mature professionals who are strongly oriented toward their work, a somewhat different value shift is occurring. They are increasingly put off by what they see as meaningless, unproductive, and demeaning rituals in the day-to-day life of the employee beholden to one organization for income and job security. They point to busy work, arbitrary performance appraisals by superiors with less technical competence, office politics, pointless meetings, gossip, and "the annual kickback to the chairman's favorite charity drive." In particular, when independent professionals explain why they left—or have never joined—the ranks of the organization man, they refer to "politics" time and again.[6] Alice McCray is one such individual. In 1986 she left a nationally known firm to start her own consulting company, A.F. McCray Consulting Services of Silver Spring, Maryland. In comparing corporate life with her role as a consultant, she notes,

> My clients treat me as a professional who is coming in to do a specific job. They don't have you doing busy work like you sometimes do as an employee because you're paid by the hour; they want to get the most out of you that they can. I don't have to go to staff meetings. The only ones I go to are the ones that pertain strictly to my work. And, I'm not in the politics or the gossip . . . which I like.

At a 1986 job fair conducted by a California firm that supplies computer professionals to Silicon Valley, some 80 percent of the résumés received were from professionals who were already employed but were looking for opportunities as freelancers.

Many professionals, as well as skilled office workers who prefer "permanent temping," are determined not to repeat the mistakes of the hundreds of thousands of white-collar employees who were fired in recent years. Soothed by top management's often-literal description of the company as "our family," those employees relied on the implied commitment of family-like loyalty through good times and bad. They made no preparation for survival outside the company. When they were let go, they found that their loyalty, and even outstanding job performance, virtually counted for nothing. For years the objects of salutary performance reviews and high praise in the annual report ("our most important assets"), they found themselves, once on the street, described as "layers of fat" that had to be trimmed lest they suffocate the organization. These victims and their surviving peers have learned that their only allegiance is to themselves, and so has the next generation of workers. The comment of one MBA student at the University of Maryland is typical: "Whatever I do, I'll never let a corporation set me up like they did my father."

In many cases, then, the increasingly professional, arm's-length association that is the basis of many alternative employment arrangements simply reflects a mutual recognition of new realities. The following chapters will explore several types of such arrangements, how they can work to the advantage of both employees and employers, and where they may fall short in meeting the expectations of either or both parties.

Notes

1. M.J. Gannon, "The Management of Peripheral Employees," *Personnel Journal*, September 1975, 482.
2. S. Prokesch, "Remaking the American C.E.O.," *New York Times*, 25 January 1987, 1F.
3. Ibid., 8F.
4. Bureau of National Affairs, Inc., *The Changing Workplace: New Directions in Scheduling and Staffing*. Special Report (Washington, D.C.: 1986), 1, 3.
5. Ibid., 5.
6. In a recent help-wanted ad in the *Washington Post*, a "job shop" which employs systems professionals for temporary assignments at client firms listed "no company politics" along with overtime premium, group health insurance, and other benefits it provides employees.

2

Temporary Workers

Temporary workers—or "temps," as they are commonly called—are engaged by a company for a fixed—and usually brief—period of time, in contrast to permanent full- and part-time staff, who have an uninterrupted employment relationship with an employer.

Although temporary workers have long been part of the work force, employers today are using them both more frequently and more broadly. In one form or another, more than 90 percent of U.S. businesses and more than 95 percent of Fortune-500 corporations now hire temporary help. While the increase in the number of temporary workers has drawn attention in the popular press, much of the related information either has been anecdotal or has been reported in diffuse sources such as government and industry databases and scholarly journals.

In May 1986, The Bureau of National Affairs, Inc. (BNA), produced a report based on their comprehensive survey of 599 private-sector employers throughout the United States. Data from 442 respondents confirmed the general trend toward increased temporary employment, as well as other alternative staffing techniques. BNA also discovered that some companies have been disappointed in these efforts. By combining aggregate data with case histories of alternative staffing arrangements in defined categories, BNA thus provided a basis by which employers can compare their staffing situations and philosophies to those of the firms queried.

The BNA survey results formed the basis for a special report, *The Changing Workplace: New Directions in Staffing and Scheduling*.[1] Data from the BNA survey and special report will be drawn on frequently in this chapter.

Categories of Temporary Workers

Temporary workers are usually hired in one of three ways: through employment with temporary help service (THS) firms, as short-term hires, and as on-call workers.

Temporary Help Service (THS) Firms

Temporary help service firms sprang up during World War II to provide the workers needed to meet peak demands and maintain vital war production when regular employees were absent. After the war, employers continued to view these "temps" as something of a necessary evil, that is, a quick, but less-than-satisfactory solution to ad hoc staffing problems. Work performed by temps was limited almost exclusively to clerical and unskilled industrial tasks. By the 1960s, "Kelly Girl" had become almost a generic term for the file clerk, switchboard operator, or secretary sent over when a regular employee was ill or on vacation. Another major THS firm chose a work glove as its logo, symbolizing the male side of the temporary help industry.

The industry has grown rapidly. According to the U.S. Bureau of Labor Statistics (BLS), the number of people employed by THS firms increased more than 400 percent—from 184,000 to 750,000—between 1970 and 1986. In 1985, an average of one in six American workers was working part time.

More than 2,200 THS firms now operate 7,000 offices throughout the country. In dollar volume, the Commerce Department has reported that temporary employment services are now the second fastest growth industry in the country. Measured in payroll (i.e., dollars paid to the temporary staffers provided to client companies), the industry has experienced a 19 percent yearly growth rate since 1970—about double the average GNP growth rate for the same period. The annual payroll of THS firms now approaches $7 billion.[2]

Although the total number of temporary workers has increased impressively, BLS data show that the number of workers supplied by THS firms was less than 1 percent of the nonagricultural work force in December 1985.[3] Consistent with that finding, BLS survey respondents indicated that agency temps accounted for an average addition of less than 1 percent to their regular work forces.

Although THS firms are commonly *called* agencies, they are not actually agencies. An agency, such as an employment agency, represents—but does not employ—the people it refers to clients. A THS firm, on the other hand, is the legal employer of the workers it supplies. Employers contracting with THS firms should avoid referring to them as "agencies," at least in official documents such as contracts or job orders, to avoid any implication that they are the legal employers of THS temps.

Because the worker is employed by the THS firm, the client is essentially relieved of the burden of recruiting, interviewing, screening, testing, and training. Most THS firms also provide performance guarantees and fidelity bonding with respect to their employees. The THS firm is responsible for payroll, bookkeeping, income and Social Security tax withholding and contributions, workers' compensation, fringe benefits, and similar costs and obligations. It also handles all related forms and government reports.

The THS firm generally charges the client a service fee expressed as a percentage of the employee's hourly wage. The markup may vary from client to client, with high-volume users paying lower fees. In a typical case in which the employee receives $5 per hour, the billing rate to the client may be $7.50 per hour.

Short-Term Hires

These individuals are typically hired for a particular project or a specified period of time or both. Included in this category are freelancers representing nearly every professional/technical field in which one finds permanent employees. Examples include programming, writing, research, and design. They are often called in to provide technical support when a company secures a major contract and does not have enough regular staff to carry through. In other cases, the short-term hire may have needed expertise that is not available internally. Because of that expertise, he or she may even direct regular staff. However, the freelancer should not be confused with a contract consultant. Contract consultants are engaged to help define and analyze problems and recommend alternative solutions; their primary product is advice. Freelance professionals called in as short-term hires complete defined tasks to company specifications.

Because of their association with job shops, freelancers are often called "shoppers." "Subway" or "freeway" shoppers work for employers in a given metropolitan area, in contrast to "road" job shoppers, who may relocate from state to state. Sometimes freelancers will market their services directly to potential clients and also be registered with one or more job shops.

Like THS firms, technical service job shops have enjoyed great success in recent years. Those providing engineering talent, for example, have grown about 30 percent per year for the last several years, and they paid some $2 billion in annual salaries in 1985. There are more than 700 such organizations throughout the country today.[4]

Although they have similar responsibilities, job shops differ from THS firms in the following respects:

- The job shop typically submits several résumés to the client, who selects the person to be hired.
- Technical assignment contracts tend to be of longer duration than those performed by THS employees; their average duration is about six months, although they can range from two months to several years.
- Job shoppers usually do not convert to regular employees of the client during the assignment or upon its completion.
- Hourly compensation tends to be 25 to 50 percent higher than that received by the client's regular staff in similar positions.
- In addition to the service fee, the client may pay a per diem, which is passed on to the employee as reimbursement for food and lodging expenses if the employee has relocated to work on the client's project.
- Contract professionals tend to be highly experienced. Adapting quickly to new environments is a skill in itself, one that is sharpened with each new assignment the professional completes.
- Some job shops will perform the client's work in their own offices; however, such "in-house" work is still a small part of technical service firms' volume.

On-Call Workers

These are people who have agreed to be more or less available to a given employer for temporary jobs as needed. A group of such workers is usually referred to as an "on-call pool," or an "in-house" pool when it is set up and administered within the company. The terms will be used interchangeably here. Many pool members are individuals who previously worked for the employer as regular staff but left the ranks under amicable terms. They may be retirees or individuals who left the employer's regular rolls because of family obligations. Finally, the on-call category includes laborers available through union hiring halls.

Patterns in Use of Temporary Employees

A 1985 survey by BNA found that 77 percent of their respondents used THS temps, 64 percent used short-term hires, and 34 percent used on-call workers.[5] In examining any such data, however, it should be borne in mind that temporary help usage fluctuates with employment levels. For example, a 1981 survey by Mayall and Nelson of 1,200 randomly selected firms in 20 standard metropolitan statistical areas (SMSAs) yielded usage rates for the three categories of temporary workers of 37.9, 32, and 16.8 percent, respectively—roughly half the rates found by BNA in 1985. Mayall and Nelson pointed out that 1981 was a year of rising unemployment, hence lower temp usage than would otherwise be the case.[6]

Many employers use more than one type of temporary employee along with regular staff. The specific category of temp to be called on to meet a particular staffing need—or the decision as to whether a temp should be called on at all—is a function of several variables. When those variables are defined and analyzed, definite patterns emerge in employer use of temporary help as an alternative staffing strategy. Except where otherwise indicated, statistics referred to here are from the BNA survey.

Task Environment

The first key variable deals with elements of the company's internal environment—the set of circumstances giving rise to the task itself. Typical factors include the following.

Special Projects

Some special projects may be planned for well in advance; others, such as gathering data for a government audit or reacting to changes mandated by a corporate acquisition, require attention on relatively short notice. In either case, a company may not have the required manpower available internally, nor find it feasible to recruit, hire, and train new employees for a project of fixed duration.

Of the employers surveyed by BNA, 70 percent cited special projects as one reason for which they hire THS temps; 56 percent of employers who use short-term hires mentioned special projects as a reason; and 51 percent cited special project work as a need filled at least in part with their on-call workers.

Absence of Regular Staff

Temporaries are often used to fill in both for scheduled absences, such as vacations and other personal leave, and for unplanned absences, such as that caused by illness or other unforeseen events. Of the firms surveyed, 75 percent of those using THS temps cited absence fill-in as a reason; 42 percent of those employing short-term hires mentioned it; and 68 percent of those using on-call workers gave it as a reason.

Interim Staffing for Vacant Positions

It typically takes five to six weeks to recruit and select an individual to fill a permanent job. Jobs requiring special skills may take months to fill. In today's staffing environment, every vacancy is scrutinized for opportunities to eliminate the position altogether. Scrutiny takes time, and in the interim, the former incumbent's work piles up.

Sixty-one percent of BNA's survey respondents cited interim staffing as a reason for using THS temps, as did 15 percent of those engaging short-term hires and 33 percent of those using on-call workers.

Seasonal Needs

A somewhat different pattern emerged from the survey with respect to employers who use temps to meet heavy workloads during busy seasons. Only 25 percent of respondents that use THS firms mentioned seasonal factors as a rationale; however, 53 percent of those that use short-term hires reported using them for that purpose, and 39 percent of those employing on-call workers gave seasonal needs as a reason.

Workload Fluctuations

Companies sometimes use temps as an alternative to recruiting and hiring employees to meet a surge in demand, only to lay them off when business turns down. Other traditional approaches in these industries include scheduling regular staff to work overtime or building inventory during slack periods and then drawing it down to meet increases in demand. How does use of temporary employees compare with overtime and inventory strategies as responses to workload changes? As shown in Figure 2.1, THS temps and short-term hires rank second and third—behind overtime—in relative importance among the BNA respondents. They are preferred over layoffs, inventory management, and several other options.

In a survey of 485 U.S. firms, Uniforce Temp Services, a firm in Hyde Park, New York, found that 35 percent of responding companies scheduled overtime for permanent staff, while 25 per-

Figure 2.1

IMPORTANCE OF SELECTED STRATEGIES TO MANAGE CHANGING WORKLOADS

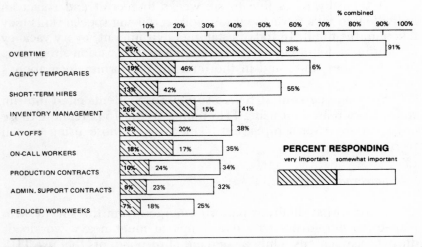

Note: Percentages are based on responses by 433 respondents who answered at least a portion of the question. Percentages do not add to 100 due to "not important," "don't know," and "not applicable" responses, and nonresponse in certain categories.

Source: The Bureau of National Affairs, Inc., *Flexible Staffing*, Exclusive Results of Survey on U.S. Firms' Use of Non-Regular Employees, Special Supplement to *BNA's Employee Relations Weekly*, 8 September 1986, 6.

cent used temps to meet peak workloads.[7] In their 1981 study, Mayall and Nelson found that work overloads, seasonal peaks, or fluctuations in demand were the reason cited by 44 percent of all respondents who used temporary workers.[8]

Need for Special Expertise

Short-term hires who are job-shop or freelance professionals are called upon for their specialized knowledge, and BNA found that on-call workers may be hired for that reason as well. A third of the companies that reported using on-call workers cited their expertise as a factor. This finding is not surprising. For many employers, the very purpose of an on-call pool is to have a cadre of workers preselected for their knowledge of the company's methods and procedures.

One area of expertise in which temporaries are used is employee training. Some THS firms do considerable training to maintain and upgrade the office automation skills of workers they seek to market to their clients. One of the case histories that follows demonstrates how, in a natural extension of that process, companies are now contracting THS firms to train regular employees in house.

Special Recruiting Circumstances

Sometimes an employer has a particular individual in mind for a temporary job but is constrained from hiring that individual directly. An example might be a retiree whose company policy prohibits re-employment, or for whom re-employment would cause loss of retirement benefits. In such a case, the employer and a THS firm might agree to an "employee transfer" or "payrolling" arrangement. Payrolling is also used to accommodate "political hires," such as employment of a relative of a major customer. Under such an agreement, the employee is recruited by the client, then put on the THS firm's payroll at a salary designated by the client. Some firms use this device to mask what are de facto permanent hires of chosen candidates during periods when regular staff are being laid off.

Strike Replacements

Some companies employ temporaries as replacements for strikers. At one time, the practice was barred under the bylaws of the

National Association of Temporary Services (NATS), a Washington-based trade association to which most major THS firms belong. Some years ago, however, the ban was struck down by the Federal Trade Commission as an illegal restraint of trade.

At least one major THS firm has adopted a position of neutrality with regard to providing services during a labor dispute. Kelly services will not increase a client's allotment of temporaries during a strike.

In 1986, several large companies used THS temps for staffing during strikes. AT&T was one such firm. By the end of a 26-day nationwide work stoppage, AT&T had 6,000 temps operating long-distance stations, and was pleased with the quality of their performance. The sensitivity of this use of temps is reflected by the fact that, in discussing with BNA his company's experience, an AT&T spokesman said he did not know which THS firms supplied the workers.

Job Categories

Across all three worker categories—THS employee, short-term hire, and on-call worker—temporaries are most often employed in office or clerical occupations. However, they are represented in nearly all occupations; for example, some THS firms specialize in placing lawyers and physicians in temporary assignments. While the 1985 BNA survey data show that there is a trend toward greater use of temporaries in professional and technical categories, they are seldom engaged in managerial or administrative jobs (see Table 2.1).

Industry Groups

The BNA survey data show significant differences among industry groups in how they match up types of temporaries with work assignments. Health care organizations that use temps are most likely to employ them in professional/technical jobs, with 33 percent using THS temps, 57 percent employing short-term hires, and 49 percent using on-call workers. Manufacturing organizations are most likely to use temporaries in production/service jobs, with 35 percent using THS temps, 57 percent using short-term hires, and 49 percent using on-call workers to fill those types of jobs. Nonmanufacturing organizations generally use temporaries in office/clerical jobs. Every user firm surveyed in the nonmanufactur-

Table 2.1

PERCENT OF USER ORGANIZATIONS USING FLEXIBLE STAFFERS IN PARTICULAR TYPES OF JOBS:

	Agency Temporaries	Short-Term Hires	On-Call Workers
Number of Companies	(336)	(277)	(159)
Managerial/Administrative	1%	5%	6%
Professional/Technical	29	38	35
Office/Clerical	96	75	63
Sales	3	5	4
Production/Service	29	44	36
Other	1	1	1

Note: Percentages are based on the number of companies using each type of flexible staffing that provided information on the occupational mix of the work performed, as shown in parentheses. "Other" includes work that could not be categorized in any of the five broad occupational classifications.

Source: The Bureau of National Affairs, Inc., *Flexible Staffing*. Exclusive Results of Survey on U.S. Firms' Use of Non-Regular Employees, Special Supplement to *BNA's Employee Relations Weekly*, 8 September 1986, 7.

ing category reported using THS temps in that way, while 85 percent used their short-term hires in office/clerical positions and 82 percent used their on-call workers for office/clerical tasks.

Size of the Organization

Larger facilities tend to use THS temps and on-call workers more frequently than smaller ones. Of executives responding to the BNA survey, 84 percent heading facilities with more than 1,000 employees reported using THS temps and 45 percent used on-call workers. Of units of less than 100 employees, however, only 64 percent reported contracting for THS temps, and only 29 percent said that they employ on-call workers. Part of the difference is that larger units are more likely to have the administrative staff and budget necessary to establish and administer an on-call pool. They may also have a personnel staff that can negotiate and coordinate with local THS suppliers and monitor the quality of their services.

Location

Out of every 10 respondents to the BNA survey from SMSAs with more than 1 million inhabitants, 9 used temporary workers;

only 46 percent of those from SMSAs with less than 100,000 inhabitants or from rural areas used them.

Union Representation

Organizations in which more than 50 percent of the eligible force is unionized were less likely to use THS temporaries, short-term hires, or on-call workers. BNA found this to be especially true with respect to short-term hires; only about 53 percent of the more heavily unionized organizations employed them versus 68 percent of those with a smaller union presence.

Case Histories

Manpower Inc.

Manpower is one example of how THS firms are using technology to help meet client needs. Manpower's sophisticated approach to training is an example of why the industry now is being relied on by companies that once were reluctant—often with good reason—to use THS temps for all but emergency staffing.

Manpower is the largest THS firm in the United States. With more than 1,000 offices in 32 countries, it employs about 700,000 workers a year; 400,000 of them work in offices as secretaries, word processor operators, and data entry personnel. U.S. sales volume for the company's fiscal year 1985 was $897 million, up from $701 million in 1984 and $572 million in 1983.

This case will focus on Manpower's employee training and pre-employment testing procedures. Manpower is by no means the only THS firm involved in training and testing, but its approach is clearly the most extensive. It has been recognized not only by clients but also by hardware and software manufacturers and independent publications that serve the office automation user community.

Manpower has IBM PCs, word processing units, and other hardware dedicated exclusively to training temps at its offices. The firm spent $5 million on purchase of IBM System/36 equipment alone, with president Mitchell Fromstein explaining that he saw the "electronic invasion" reaching the office workplace:

> We looked at the changes sweeping through the workplace
> and knew we had to retool our work force, or the market was

going to pass us by. The days when a secretary walking into a new office could just flip the "on" button, roll in a fresh sheet of letterhead, and go—are gone.

The National Association of Temporary Services confirms that word processing personnel represent the fastest growing segment of the industry.

Manpower Inc. has an annual employee turnover rate of 35 percent—about par for the industry. Recouping its initial and ongoing training investment was obviously a critical factor. The company ruled out charging the potential temp employee who might enroll in training in order to get an assignment.

Conventional training was considered uneconomical. It can take up to a week and from $400 to $800 to train a single employee. Classroom computer training is often supported by technical, jargon-laden "user manuals." Candidates for temporary jobs are often re-entry workers who left the work force to raise families. Many of them suffer from what Fromstein calls "technophobia," the fear that they could never master a complicated-looking computer terminal. They tend to be uncomfortable in a traditional classroom setting.

In answer to these concerns, Manpower developed its own copyrighted training software, called Skillware. These are tutorial diskettes that allow trainees either to learn from scratch or brush up skills on specific hardware and software. The company has packages for hardware systems such as the IBM PC, Wang, IBM Displaywriter, CPT, NBI, DEC, and IBM System/36; popular software applications include Multimate, Lotus 1-2-3, dBase III, and WordStar 2000. Diskettes in seven foreign languages are used in Manpower's overseas offices. Skillware is interactive, self-paced, and puts the trainee through "live" exercises. In contrast to traditional programmed tutorials, it allows the trainee to actually create, edit, and print a document, rather than simply simulate those critical functions. The instructions are presented in nontechnical, informal language. Trainees may repeat sections in which they encounter problems. Manpower claims that in one day a person with no word processing experience can learn enough of the basics of document creation, editing, and printing to receive an assignment.

Employees can progress from beginner to intermediate and advanced levels, for which they are tested and certified. Because the Skillware diskettes are similar in approach, training time can decrease as much as 50 percent as a trainee works through lessons on different equipment and software.

At the completion of training on a given system, the employee receives a pocket-sized support manual for reference on the job. Commenting on the handiness of these manuals, one employee pointed out that "so many times the client has lost the original manual for the word processor, and even the regular employees do not know how to perform a certain function."[9]

Some 85,000 Manpower employees have been trained on Skillware at an average cost to Manpower of about $100 per person. To meet the continuing demand for temporaries with office automation skills, Fromstein hopes to increase Manpower's annual training volume to 150,000 employees, which he estimates would drive down the training cost to about $30 per person. Sally Crawford, president of Crawford and Associates, Inc., of Bloomingdale, Illinois, has noted that even at $100 per person Manpower's training is a bargain. Her firm specializes in office systems training in five states and charges $99 per person for a half-day standard word-processing class. The firm charges $70 per hour for instruction of one or two people at a client's site; certain courses such as dedicated Xerox word processing require 12 hours of instruction.

Vista Chemical Company

Manpower's training expertise has led to joint efforts with major clients. One such effort involved Vista Chemical Company, headquartered in Houston, Texas. According to Cheryl Parker, systems administrator responsible for staff training at headquarters, four sales offices, and seven plants, the company became interested when Manpower announced completion of Skillware for the IBM 5520 in late 1984. Vista had just installed such a system at Houston. It also used IBM Displaywriter and Xerox 860 word processors, for which Manpower already had Skillware diskettes.

Manpower, however, did not have a 5520 in Houston because it was too expensive to install at a local office. Therefore Vista and Manpower agreed to cross-train their employees. Manpower would train Vista operators on site, and in exchange, Vista would allow Manpower to use the 5520 system to train its temps. The arrangement was beneficial to Parker, who previously had to set aside three or four days for training each new operator. With Manpower doing the on-site training, she had more time to plan and coordinate the overall training effort. Parker says that if it were necessary she would pay for Manpower's in-house training directly, rather than through the barter arrangement.

Manpower has established procedures for evaluating the skills of employees before offering them assignments. Two kinds of tests are administered to each applicant. One is a recognition and proficiency test to measure word processing knowledge on a specific system such as Wang or Xerox. The second, called "Ultraskill," is a work-sample test in which the candidate must create, edit, and type a document from a handwritten or machine-dictated draft. Eight basic clerical skills are measured: spelling, punctuation, following instructions, editing, formatting, proofing, machine transcription, and speed.

To ensure that its testing program is an effective selection tool and that it meets federal nondiscrimination requirements, the company based it on a job analysis involving employees and supervisors in client companies. After skill requirements were defined and prototype instruments pretested and debugged, tests were administered to a sample of employees. The results were correlated with supervisory ratings to establish criterion validity in accordance with Equal Employment Opportunity Commission (EEOC) Uniform Selection Guidelines.

Manpower shares its measurement methods and terminology with its clients, so that they speak the same language when discussing the skill mix required for a given job assignment (see Exhibits 2.1 and 2.2).

Manpower is now Vista's main supplier of temporary help. Parker comments that the company has never assigned an employee who did not meet the specified skill level. She also likes the operator support manuals referred to earlier; she finds them more up to date than the vendor-supplied manuals.[10]

Manpower has, on occasion, assisted companies such as Miller Brewing and Xerox Corporation in training regular clerical and field sales staffs with Skillware diskettes. The company stresses that these were goodwill gestures that may lead to increased temporary placements through favorable publicity. Manpower does not sell the Skillware diskettes.

However, the company now sends "temporary training administrators" (TTAs) to major clients who want assistance in training their permanent employees. The TTA brings Skillware diskettes to the client's office, sets them up, and remains on hand to answer questions as permanent employees work through the exercises. Again, the assistance is an indirect marketing tool: the goal is to increase the customer's confidence in Manpower's ability to provide personnel who are at least as well trained as regular staff.

Exhibit 2.1

TEMPORARY SERVICES

MANPOWER'S GUIDE TO
WORD PROCESSING PROFICIENCY LEVELS
APPLICATION CHART

The following chart is a description of various word processing **applications (or types of documents)** defined by the functions necessary to produce those documents. Applications and functions are described in universal (non-machine specific) terms.

These applications and their accompanying functions are expressed in terms of three proficiency levels. Manpower has identified these levels of proficiency or capability for word processing operators: Basic, Intermediate and Advanced.

The following examples illustrate **Manpower's** definition of the word processing activities that fall into each proficiency level.

APPLICATIONS (DOCUMENTS)	FUNCTIONS USED TO PRODUCE THESE DOCUMENTS	DESIRED PROF. LEVEL B = Basic I = Intermediate A = Advanced
LETTERS/MEMOS ORIGINAL, ONE-OF-A-KIND LETTERS	Set up system; create document from handwritten, rough copy or machine dictation; make minor edits; store and print on letterhead	B
INDIVIDUAL FORM (REPETITIVE) LETTERS/ DOCUMENTS WITH STOP CODES	Set up system; create original letter/document from handwritten, rough copy or machine dictation; insert "stop codes" where unique information will be inserted; fill in blanks of each letter/document by typing in variable information like names, addresses, balance due, dates, etc.; make minor edits; store and print on letterhead (examples: past due notices, contracts, rental agreements, etc.)	B
LABELS AND ENVELOPES	Set up system; set envelope/label format; insert "variable instruction" where each name and address will be inserted; merge lists of names and addresses with envelope/label format; store and print	I
STANDARD LETTERS MERGED WITH VARIABLE LISTS/DOCUMENTS	Set up system; create standard letter from handwritten, rough copy or machine dictation; insert "variable instructions" where unique information will be inserted; merge documents with list(s) of variables; make edits to standard letter necessary to accommodate "merged" information; store and/or print on letterhead (examples: standard reply letters, mass mailings, etc.)	I
STANDARD LETTERS SELECTIVELY MERGED WITH FILES OR DATA BASES	Set up system; create standard letter from handwritten, rough copy or machine dictation; insert "file merge" instructions where file data will be inserted; sort and select appropriate records to be merged; make edits and format changes necessary to accommodate "merged" data; store and/or print on letterhead (examples: mass mailings to **selected** recipients, i.e. customers in a certain region; suppliers of certain products; prospects of a specific size; by zip code for bulk mailing postage discounts; etc.)	A
FORMS FILL-IN FORMS	Set up system; retrieve stored form; fill in blanks by typing in variable information; make minor edits; store and print on pre-printed forms (examples: insurance claims, purchase orders, questionnaires, applications, etc.)	B
NEW FORMS	Set up system; create form format; type in variable information; make edits; store and print (examples: report forms, applicant logs, etc.)	I
MULTI-PAGE DOCUMENTS REPORTS	Set up system; create document from handwritten, rough copy or machine dictation; copy and/or move text within document; paginate, hyphenate, justify text; make minor edits; store and print	B
ASSEMBLED DOCUMENTS	Set up system; create new text; retrieve and assemble blocks of stored text (boilerplate); reformat; do major editing and revising; store and print	I
PROPOSALS AND STUDIES	Set up system; create document from handwritten, rough copy or machine dictation; use headers and footers, automatic page numbering and outlining; copy and move text from other stored documents; do major editing and revising, including deleting and replacing blocks of text; set up multi-columns (these documents often include charts and tables); store and print	I
MANUALS AND HANDBOOKS WITH DUAL COLUMN TEXT (NEWSPAPER FORMAT)	Set up system; create document from handwritten, rough copy or machine dictation; use headers and footers, automatic page numbering and outlining; copy and move text from other stored documents; set up multi-columns (these documents often include charts and tables); do major editing and revising, including inserting, deleting and replacing blocks of text and moving columns; format dual-column text; use keystroke memory features; store and print	A
STATISTICAL DOCUMENTS ORIGINAL TEXT DOCUMENTS CONTAINING CHARTS AND TABLES	Set up system; create document from handwritten, rough copy or machine dictation; set up columns; insert, delete, move and replace columns; align decimals; center headings over columns; store and print (example: lengthy documents containing profit and loss statements and balance sheets, like annual reports)	I
TEXT DOCUMENTS INTEGRATED WITH SPECIAL SOFTWARE	Set up system; create text surrounding charts/tables; integrate spreadsheet data; calculate row and column totals; reformat as needed; store and print (examples: sales forecasts, budgets, etc.)	A
RECORDS/LIST PROCESSING (WORKING WITH DATA BASES) ADDRESS LISTS	Set up system; access records processing or load data base program; instruct the system to sort and select specific records and then create a list of requested information; send this new document to file, to print, or both	A
REPORT GENERATION	Set up system; create document from handwritten, rough copy or machine dictation; access records processing or load data base program; instruct the system to sort and select specific file information; compile it into a data report and merge that report — at a specific point — into the text document; send this system-generated report to file, to print, or both; edit and reformat the report now inside the "merged" document as needed; store and print the final document	A

Source: Reprinted by permission of Manpower Inc.

Exhibit 2.2

MANPOWER'S GUIDE TO
WORD PROCESSING PROFICIENCY LEVELS
FUNCTION CHART

The following chart is a detailed listing of word processing **functions** described in universal (non-machine specific) terms.

Manpower has also identified three levels of proficiency or capability for word processing operators: Basic, Intermediate and Advanced. The functions below are expressed in terms of the three proficiency levels. They illustrate **Manpower's** definition of word processing functions that fall into each level.

BASIC	INTERMEDIATE	ADVANCED
A BASIC OPERATOR CAN:	**AN INTERMEDIATE OPERATOR CAN EXECUTE ALL BASIC FUNCTIONS AND CAN:**	**AN ADVANCED OPERATOR CAN EXECUTE ALL BASIC AND INTERMEDIATE FUNCTIONS AND CAN:**
SET UP THE SYSTEM • turn machine on and off • load system/program diskette • load work diskette • use operator I.D. and password (security codes) • prepare/initialize/format diskettes • access word processing from hard disk or shared system **KEYBOARD (TYPE)** • use alpha and numeric keys (keyboard familiarity) • use code and function keys (underscore, center, boldface, etc.) • use cursor or locator keys **CREATE DOCUMENTS** • name documents • format (set tabs, margins, line spacing, pitch, etc.) • use prompts, messages and menus • use stop codes (with repetitive documents) • paginate/repaginate • hyphenate • justify text • use spell check features • correct characters and words while keyboarding **MAKE MINOR EDITS** • scroll (horizontally and vertically) to review text • change margins, tabs, line spacing, etc. • delete, insert and replace text (characters, words and lines) • copy or move text (within a document) **STORE/FILE TEXT** • store newly created documents • store more than one version of a document • set up and maintain text files **RECALL/RETRIEVE TEXT** • use document index/directory • access stored text/documents • access ("go to") specific pages/sections within a document **PRINT TEXT** • start/stop printer • set up printer using menus or print commands to print from screen or storage • load paper • modify print queues • change ribbons or print wheels • operate automatic sheet feeder • cancel print request • print specific pages or text segments	**CREATE DOCUMENTS** • use automatic page numbering features • set up multi-column text (as in a table or chart) • use footnotes • use headers and footers • use decimal alignment • use subscripts and superscripts • use outline features • work with proportionally-spaced text (formatting, setting up tables, etc.) • merge standard documents (form letters) with variable lists • create libraries/folders • use alternate (stored) formats **DO MAJOR EDITING AND REVISING** • reformat documents (margins, tabs, etc.) • move or copy/duplicate blocks of text or documents (from document to document or diskette to diskette) • delete, insert or replace blocks of text • move or copy columns • delete, insert or replace columns • delete documents (from library/storage) • use global search and replace • use document/paragraph assembly features (boilerplates) **SPECIAL FUNCTIONS AND SYSTEM MAINTENANCE TASKS** • perform general housekeeping (archive, delete multiple documents, etc.) • use a laser printer • work with DOS commands • use directories	**USE SPECIAL FEATURES AND SOFTWARE PACKAGES** • use math features • sort and select (Records/List Processing or work with Data Bases) • set up and maintain data files • merge with files • use communication features • write Glossary, Keystroke Save, or other keystroke memory routines or macros • create and work with dual column text (newspaper format) • create system dictionary • use file conversion features **PERFORM OTHER SPECIALIZED FUNCTIONS** • use graphics • perform system troubleshooting • write special programs • convert documents to ASCII • integrate different software packages (spreadsheet with word processing, etc.) • interface with photocomposition and typesetting equipment, scanning and facsimile devices, etc. **PERFORM LEAD OPERATOR FUNCTIONS** • supervise other operators • set up and revise system profiles • set up printer and workstation profiles • assign security codes • manage system housekeeping (purge files, make backup copies of documents, archive, etc.)

Source: Reprinted by permission of Manpower Inc.

Bank of America

In August 1985, Bank of America implemented an on-call employee pool, ending a long-standing reliance on THS firms, which had supplied as many as 800 temporary workers a month. Approximately 250 "B of A temps," as they are called, are now employed there for special projects, absence fill-in, and peak-load assistance. According to Addie Johnson, Manager of Staffing Services, B of A had two primary reasons for this major decision:

1. Operational and quality control. Management officials felt that the temp firms had become "more entrenched than they should be" in the bank and that there was a need to regain control of staffing. In addition to the efficiencies that might be gained through closer control, B of A was aware that, as a bank, it had to be especially sensitive to public perceptions of its control over employee selection and supervision.
2. Cost savings. Bank management determined that before an in-house program could be approved, the human resources department would have to demonstrate that it would yield a net cost savings compared to THS firm usage.

In the first year of the in-house plan, the company exceeded its target for significant reduction of THS costs. Bank of America also feels that its on-call workers are more committed and productive than THS temps.

Part of the savings come from using funds that would otherwise go toward THS service fees to attract a higher caliber of employee. Although the company declines to give specific figures, it offers a hypothetical example of a word processor operator. A THS firm might bill the client $17 per hour for the employee's services, paying the employee $11 of that amount. In the absence of a THS firm, the employer could offer operators $12 to $13 per hour and apply the remaining $4 to $5 in savings to administrative costs. B of A has found that the savings vary with supply and demand for workers in various skill categories.

As an additional tool to recruit and retain well-qualified temps, the company designed a compensation plan that provides merit-based step increases. Several other factors also have contributed to attracting and retaining quality performers for the on-call pool. First, B of A has a high temporary-to-permanent conversion ratio—in excess of 20 percent. Second, and closely related to the conversion ratio, is the bank's no-layoff policy with respect to regular employees. Clearly, then, a person seeking regular employment has a strong incentive to enter the B of A program.

Temporary-to-permanent conversions can reduce recruiting and turnover costs, and without the involvement of a THS firm, Bank of America has more control over both the "try" and the "buy" side. Johnson notes, however, that she does not expect the conversion rate to exceed 20 percent because there are "many, many people who do not want to be tied to a corporation."

This reflects to some extent the cultural ambience of the Bay Area. Many of the bank's temporaries are "freelance kinds of individuals" seeking careers in the arts. They are adept at such tasks as word processing and data entry, and they support themselves with temporary work between stage calls and art exhibitions. The first B of A temp was, in fact, an actor who became a proficient word processor and secretary. The company is careful to note that in a region with different life-styles and demographics an in-house temp program might not be as successful as its San Francisco effort.

Johnson reports that most of the bank's temporaries prefer working there to working for THS firms. They describe THS firm assignments as a "cattle-call" process, referring to the uncertainty as to where they will be working from one week to the next. THS temping also requires them to adjust to varying company environments. The Bank of America temps, Johnson says, can work at any company location and find that procedures are basically the same. "We can offer them temp work with a degree of continuity they can't get from an agency." One on-call temp who had moved to Los Angeles was immediately hired for temporary work there because of his experience with the bank in San Francisco. Although Bank of America temps do not receive the employee benefits offered by some THS firms, Johnson feels that the bank's overall approach has made it quite competitive without sacrificing selectivity. "If someone isn't working out [as a temp], we get that person off the rolls quickly."

Maintaining and operating a successful in-house pool requires the employer to recruit, select, and deploy a cadre of reliable workers and administer all other personnel functions connected with it. Before the final decision to go ahead, B of A carefully analyzed the expected, incremental costs attendant to such an initiative. Johnson's salary is allocated to the program. She has a subordinate manager who oversees day-to-day administration and several coordinators to maintain liaison with the on-call workers and hiring managers. By redistributing workloads, the bank has been able to administer the program without a net increase in staff hours. The company notes that administering THS arrangements requires staff time, too, especially when multiple suppliers are involved.

The program is now being extended to Bank of America offices in Los Angeles, and it is being considered for its Pasadena facilities. (Other aspects of the Bank of America temp program will be discussed later in this chapter—see "THS Firms Versus the On-call Pool.")

Jobs Unlimited

Jobs Unlimited is a job shop located in San Jose, California. It supplies technical and professional personnel to the high-technology firms located in that area's Silicon Valley. Like most job shops, it remains the legal employer of the shoppers it has on assignment to its clients, but has no formal tie to them when they are not on assignment. The inactive shoppers remain on a roster for consideration for further assignments. Jobs Unlimited's clients usually agree not to offer permanent employment to a shopper during the first 90 days of the assignment. After that, the company may contract directly with the individual.

Apple Computer, Inc.

Apple Computer, Inc., is a Jobs Unlimited client that relies on a number of temporaries in occupations ranging from highly technical to lower-skilled assembly work. Cost savings are not a factor, according to Lamont Monroe, human resources liaison for the 4,700-employee computer maker. In BNA's 1985 special report, he noted that the temps' pay scales are the same as for regular employees and that the markups of temp suppliers are about equal to the cost of employee benefits. The benefits to Apple are

- access to qualified individuals in a range of disciplines;
- ability to adjust staffing levels quickly; and
- ability to evaluate temporaries for their possible fit as regular employees.

Apple contracts with a number of job shops and is careful to communicate just what it seeks in employees assigned to it. The company's Fremont, California, office brings in temporaries under a 60-day-review plan. The 60-day reviews reinforce to the temps that they are indeed there on a temporary basis and have no assurance of working into permanent positions.

Apple is particularly concerned about the possibility of having a temporary employee planted by a competitor to discover proprietary information and plans. Because Apple has a highly participative management style—even seeking worker input on new products and marketing strategies—the concern is all the more acute. The company relies on its temporary help suppliers to do at least routine screening of candidates for assignment there.

Like other technical job shops, Jobs Unlimited is diversifying. By supplying temporary employees in more traditional clerical roles, it hopes both to increase its value to its customers and to provide a hedge against the ups and downs of the high-tech job market.

Travelers Corporation

In 1981, Travelers developed a pool of on-call retired employees to help meet a continuous need for temporary workers at their Hartford, Connecticut, national headquarters, where some 10,000 people are employed. The on-call retirees range in age from 55 to 84. On any given day, 175 of them are at work at the Hartford offices, filling about 70 percent of the temporary job vacancies. Outside temporaries fill the balance of the temporary jobs, most often in positions in which technology has advanced since the former incumbents retired.[11] To deal with that problem, however, the company has begun paid training programs for retirees who wish to update their skills. Some of those programs are geared toward advanced skills such as using computer software. Paid training in such basic skills as typing is also offered for annuitants who wish to brush up.

The temporaries usually fill in for absent workers and help during peak periods such as year-end closeout of financial records. The jobs include such traditional office positions as clerk, data processing operator, and accountant. Hourly pay for the retirees is at the midpoint of the salary range of each job being filled. This amounts to more than the retiree would earn as an employee of a temporary service firm, but less than the fee a temporary firm would charge Travelers. The retirees receive health benefits from their retirement plans, and Travelers provides no other health or welfare benefits to them.

While the concept and operation of the annuitant pool are similar to those of other employers, Travelers has taken additional steps to augment it and make it more flexible. First, the company has recruited retirees from other firms. Although these account for about half of the 600 retirees now active in the program, Travelers calls on its own pensioners more frequently. Second, it has instituted job-sharing among the on-call workers, with 38 retirees now sharing jobs. For example, 16 annuitants share 4 jobs that involve answering customer telephone inquiries. "They do the job better than anyone else we ever had do the job," says Georgina Lucas, administrator of Travelers' Older Americans program. "They know our products and services, understand the company, and have excellent interpersonal skills."[12]

The company's policy allows retirees to work up to 960 hours a year without loss of pension benefits. However, a Social Security provision penalizes retired workers one dollar for every two dollars earned after they reach a maximum income level. Travelers has found, as have others, that this earnings cap effectively discourages retirees' participation in the on-call program after they have reached that point, even though they may not have reached Travelers' maximum of 960 hours.

Federal Government

Many government operations are seasonal or cyclical. The Internal Revenue Service, for example, has heavy staffing needs from January through April, when tax returns are being filed. The Census Bureau of the Commerce Department builds up staff in preparation for the population count that is taken each decade. Temporary workers play a role in filling these peak-load staffing needs.

In 1984, the U.S. Office of Personnel Management (OPM) issued regulations covering three categories of other than full-time permanent employees: seasonal, on-call, and intermittent. The regulations outline the benefits and service credits to which they are entitled. In 1985, OPM added other provisions for temporary employees.

Seasonal Employees

These employees work for recurring periods of less than 12 months a year, but are eligible for health and life insurance benefits throughout the year. When not working, they are in nonduty/nonpay status and subject to recall. During these periods, seasonal employees are generally free to accept employment in the federal government or elsewhere. Sometimes the government is able to assign seasonal workers to other work in the same agencies when their seasonal projects are completed.

OPM encourages federal supervisors to work seasonal employees at least six months out of the year to minimize the cost of unearned service credit and benefits. It does not recommend, however, that they be employed as substitutes for full-time staff. Benefits for seasonal employees are not inexpensive; they include life and health insurance and up to six months of credit for retirement while in nonpay status.

On-Call Employees

In contrast to seasonal employees, on-call workers work on and off throughout the year, rather than continuously during a set period. They are called on to handle peak loads as an alternative to excessive overtime. They are covered by the civil service retirement system, and because they are expected to work at least six months per year they are eligible for health and life insurance throughout the year if they pay their share of the premiums.

OPM reports that one difficulty of administering the on-call pool lies in tracking the movements of these workers in and out of duty status. Release and recall of on-call employees must conform to specific procedures that recognize job performance and seniority.

Intermittent Employees

The government employs intermittents to respond to sporadic and unpredictable events; snow removal is an example. They generally are not eligible for health or life insurance coverage and are eligible for retirement coverage only if serving under a career or career-conditional appointment. They do not earn annual or sick leave.

Temporary Employees

Federal agencies may make and extend temporary appointments, which are defined as nonpermanent employment, for a specified time of one year or less. These appointments may be renewed for four consecutive years of service.

In a memo to federal agencies, OPM stated,

> Temporary employment is one extremely important element in a comprehensive staffing policy, and one which is very cost efficient. This type of employment gives agencies flexibility to deal with workload peaks and at the same time can be used to protect the jobs of career employees who are serving in activities facing cutbacks. [13]

The government uses temporaries for such purposes as filling jobs that may be contracted out or filling vacancies in positions into which permanent workers may someday be "bumped" when their own positions are eliminated.

OPM raised the highest job grade for which temporaries could be hired from GS-7 to GS-12, making it possible for agencies to hire professional temporaries.

According to Cherlyn S. Granrose and Eileen Applebaum, professors at Temple University, OPM has reported that the federal government filled more than 244,000 jobs with temporary workers in 1984.

Advantages and Disadvantages of Temporary Staffing

As noted in Chapter 1, employee desires are partly responsible for the growth of the contingent work force. Changing attitudes about work and family, employment relationships, and career and personal goals all play a part. However, some members of the contingent work force do not participate as a result of choice or a dispassionate weighing of pros and cons. They need the work.

For the employer, the benefits of alternative employment strategies include

- cost savings;
- flexibility;
- obviating the need for increases in regular staff;
- increased productivity; and
- effective application of expertise.

These employer rationales are, like employee motivations, often intertwined. Bringing one job shopper on board might meet each of these employer concerns to some degree; but in another set of circumstances engaging that shopper for the same job might not be as advantageous as employing a regular worker.

The case histories discussed earlier showed how specific companies, as well as the federal government, have employed temporary workers to best meet these criteria. A broader review of the advantages and disadvantages of employing temporary workers follows.

Cost Savings

Pay and Benefits

The 1985 BNA survey respondents indicated that temps were more or less costly than regular staff depending on the category of temporary worker employed—THS temp, short-term hire, or on-call pool. For example, 41 percent of companies found THS temps to be costlier, 30 percent found them to cost approximately the same, and only 27 percent found them less costly (see Table 2.2).

The THS industry believes that employers often underestimate the true cost of wages and benefits for full-time employees. According to the U.S. Chamber of Commerce, employing a person at a salary of $200 per week requires $85.64 per week, or 42 percent, of additional employer expenses. One-time hiring costs represent 7 percent, and pay for time not worked represents 9

Table 2.2

HOURLY PAY AND BENEFITS COST OF FLEXIBLE STAFFERS
COMPARED WITH REGULAR EMPLOYEES

	Agency Temporaries	Short-Term Hires	On-Call Workers
Number of Companies	(339)	(282)	(161)
"Generally higher"	41%	6%	11%
"Generally lower"	27	59	42
"Generally about the same"	30	32	45
Other	3	3	3

Source: The Bureau of National Affairs, Inc., *Flexible Staffing*. Exclusive Results of Survey on U.S. Firms' Use of Non-Regular Employees, Special Supplement to *BNA's Employee Relations Weekly*, 8 September 1986, 7.

percent of salary. Time not worked includes holidays, vacations, paid personal leave, and paid tardiness and absences. These costs total more than $33 per week for the $200-per-week employee. While most employers include mandatory taxes and insurance and the cost of company-paid benefits in calculating total hourly costs, many tend to overlook these significant "hidden costs" of recruiting and maintaining a permanent work force.

Specific figures will vary from case to case, but such examples make it clear that comparison of per-hour costs between regular and temporary employees must be based on the number of hours during which employees are actually on the job—not on hours paid. For example, analysis of the Chamber of Commerce figures reveals that 21 percent of the potential savings from using temporaries lies in elimination of pay for time not worked—the variable that is most often overlooked. Proper accounting for time not worked is closely tied to the broad concept of productivity, which will be addressed later in this chapter.

Recruitment and Employment Costs

Many employers find the temporary employment relationship an ideal way to "try and buy" permanent staff by offering employment to individuals who have proved their worth on the job as THS temps or job shoppers. While few of the BNA survey respondents said they intentionally hire temps with this in mind, 62 percent of the THS users, 55 percent of those using short-term hires, and 41 percent of those using on-call workers said they occasionally hire those workers into regular jobs. A spokesman for Johnson and Johnson Products Company notes that many of its regular employees have entered the company by way of temporary assignments.

In the THS industry, such arrangements are called T-to-P, that is, temporary-to-permanent conversions. To the extent that T-to-P conversions transfer the risk of improper employee selection to the THS firm or job shop, the client avoids or minimizes recruiting and employment costs. Recruiting is expensive. It is estimated that the cost of recruiting, selecting, hiring, and retaining a data processing professional can amount to 60 percent of the first year's salary. For a $35,000-per-year employee, that's $21,000. If the employee is hired through an employment agency, the employer typically pays a 35-percent service fee, or $12,250. If the company relocates the new employee, it can expect to pay, on average, about $37,000 in relocation expenses. These figures do not include training costs. In high cost, tight labor market areas, salaries and recruiting expenses can run much higher. Pacific Bell, for example, estimates that it costs $110,000 to recruit, hire, and train a new programmer.

Recruiting is so expensive that a manager who hires a professional only to find that he or she is not working out may, in fact, decide not to fire that employee. Cathy Ann Connelly, president of Cathy Ann Connelly Communications, a Los Angeles consulting firm, points out that the manager in such a situation cannot easily go to management and explain his $100,000 mistake.

> He starts to contemplate the staff time already wasted during the hiring of the employee, not to mention actual money spent. He adds up advertising costs, orientation/training costs, the weeks spent looking for the employee, the employee startup costs and benefit costs.[14]

It is not uncommon for such managers to struggle along with a less-than-competent employee rather than face the alternative of starting the recruitment process anew. When management does terminate the employee, there is the ever-increasing risk of a civil suit for unjust dismissal and/or legal action under a multitude of state and federal antidiscrimination statutes and regulations.

Costly selection errors work in the other direction as well; the best technicians sometimes write the worst résumés. Such individuals may be screened out at the first step by a personnel staffer who has only a surface understanding of technical requirements and cannot read between the lines of a potentially good prospect's résumé. Well-qualified candidates who are selected for interviews may be screened out by managers who are untrained as interviewers. In other cases, the lack of interviewing skill may cause qualified candidates to reject employment offers, while admitting those who are less qualified but more adept at résumé writing.

While employers can virtually eliminate this dilemma through a "try-and-buy" approach, some THS firms actively discourage T-to-P conversions. Because their employees are their primary assets and replacing them is a financial burden, THS firms and job shops typically include in their contracts a liquidated damages clause. This clause states that a client's hiring of a THS worker within some period after termination of the temporary assignment—often 90 days—constitutes breach of contract. In such case, the contract calls for payment to the THS firm of a "release payment" of a specified amount. Kelly Services, for example, charges employers $500 each time they hire a Kelly employee directly.

In practice, THS firms often waive payment of the release fee. They argue that a temp who is disposed to take a permanent job will do so eventually, and that long-term client goodwill weighs against obstructing a client that wishes to convert a temp to permanent employment. Some THS firms and job shops actually encourage clients to engage their employees on a "try-and-buy" basis. Commercial Programming Systems (CPS), Los Angeles, is a "lease-for-hire" firm that makes telecommunications specialists available to clients on just such a basis. According to CPS president Alan Strong, clients typically extend offers to professionals he has provided after a trial period of nine months. CPS then acts as an intermediary between employee and client and charges the client no special fee. Bill Hand, an assistant general manager for the city of Los Angeles, a CPS client, comments that telecommunications professionals are "not out there in droves. We can't always find them through normal personnel channels. There is definitely an advantage to being able to convert people to regular employment at the end of the evaluation period."[15]

Because of differing supplier policies regarding "try and buy," employers should be sure to reach an understanding on that subject before engaging their services.

A variation of THS-firm and job-shop usage called "employee transfer" or "payrolling" was discussed earlier. In those cases, the client recruits the employee, then directs a THS firm or job shop to hire that person, thus becoming the employer for legal purposes. The client typically determines the rate of pay. The THS firm markup is lower than normal because the client has absorbed the cost of recruitment and selection. Mayall and Nelson found that rates for such payroll servicing were often negotiated down to 15 to 22 percent, "to a point scarcely higher than the cost of mandatory services."[16] In this case, the client does not save recruitment costs, but does save the expenses of hiring and personnel administration that would be incurred in a direct hire.

Hiring Delays

Direct recruitment and hiring costs do not measure the true cost of filling jobs. In theory, a job exists only because it returns more to net profits than its cost. Each day that a job goes unfilled, therefore, represents a loss to the employer. In practical terms, losses can be severe: project deadlines are missed, contract bids are lost, current customers and new business are lost. In extreme cases, systems, operations, and entire ventures break down or lose money because precious weeks and months are devoted to finding and wooing candidates for permanent positions. Productivity declines as frustrated employees are "borrowed" to work extra hours on unfamiliar tasks to cover the vacant position. By the time the newcomer arrives and is oriented, he or she will be less than fully productive because of the backlog of work.

A THS firm or specialized job shop can usually have a fully qualified individual at the employer's site within one to three days. A large company in Washington, D.C., recently needed a statistical typist who could speak Portuguese; a temporary service firm came up with one in four hours. On-call pools can also produce quick results, although they tend to be limited to transient situations such as peak workloads or unexpected absences of regular staff.

Unemployment Insurance

Mandatory employer contributions to unemployment insurance funds are, for the most part, experienced-rated. When permanent employees are let go, they qualify for unemployment benefits, and future premiums paid by the employer may increase as a percentage of payroll. An increase of only 0.5 percent on a million-dollar payroll amounts to $5,000 per year in additional premiums. These premium adjustments often come at a time when the employer is least able to absorb them, since a large reduction in force usually reflects reduced profitability and cash flow.

Workload Management

Few companies can staff so that the work hours available exactly match the hours of work to be done at any one time. Staff planning is especially difficult in office settings, as compared to production environments where goods are manufactured against current and backlogged orders and inventory can be built in anticipation of new orders. When flexible staff are not used, employers often schedule overtime during peak periods, and they at least tacitly encourage employees to "stretch" the work during slack periods. In some cases, workers are forced or encouraged to take vacation when business volume is low. In the past, the tendency was toward overstaffing. In slack times, managers pursued the idle-time strategies just noted and relied on Parkinson's Law—that as the time available to do work increases, the volume of work increases to fill it. They preferred taking these approaches to being caught shorthanded in the face of workload increases. Companies also had another reason for overstaffing: Management job evaluation plans typically award more points (hence higher salary grades) to positions responsible for greater numbers of staff and payroll dollars.

Today's sweeping payroll cuts have changed things considerably. But because cuts are often panic reactions, hastily implemented, the work force reductions are not thoughtfully matched with workload reductions. The result has been a shift toward understaffing.

Temporary workers are increasingly seen as a partial, if not ideal, solution to both underuse and overuse of permanent staff. In *White-Collar Productivity*, consultant Robert N. Lehrer provided a useful model for evaluating the tradeoffs involved.[17] To demonstrate the model, he posited a work group of 150 permanent employees, which, in a typical year, has peak-load requirements of 220 employees and a "valley" requiring only 110. He added a third dimension by assuming that there are 10 dull, repetitive jobs in this work group (referred to as "unpleasant" jobs), and made the following additional assumptions:

1. Permanent employees are paid at $5.00 per hour.
2. Benefit costs of permanent employees are 33 percent of base pay.
3. Overtime premium is 50 percent of base pay.
4. Additional benefits and payroll costs attributable to overtime are 15 percent of base pay.
5. THS temps will be 15 percent more productive than permanent employees in the unpleasant jobs.

Based on these assumptions, Lehrer suggested that the permanent work force could be cut by 50 percent, to a core force of 100 employees. Ten THS employees would be working in the unpleasant jobs at any given time, providing the total complement of 110 needed to meet minimum workload requirements. Workload increases above the 110-person minimum would be handled by additional THS temps on an as-needed basis. The annual savings from such an approach, based on the model of 150 permanent employees, break down as follows:

Reducing overtime premium	$ 79,050
Eliminating idle time	262,600
Increasing productivity in unpleasant jobs	39,000
	$380,650

In this example, the hiring costs associated with the 50 permanent employees, who could arguably be replaced with temps, were treated as costs already incurred by the company. Applying the Chamber of Commerce survey finding that hiring costs for clerical employees are about 7 percent of salary, the cost of hiring those 50 employees at $10,400 each per year ($5.00 per hour × 40 hours × 52 weeks), would be $36,400. Had management planned for a mix of core employees and temps as suggested by Lehrer, it would have avoided that $36,400 expense in addition to realizing the annual savings just shown. (Lehrer's 1982 figures were developed before The Immigration Reform Act of 1987, which requires employers to verify the citizenship status of all new hires. This legislation adds another cost to the hiring process.) Except for the fact that they usually are not hired simply to take over unpleasant jobs, use of short-term hires and on-call workers can provide savings similar to those realized through temporary help services.

Bringing in supplemental, temporary workers exactly when—but only when—needed is similar to the concept of "just-in-time" inventory management of raw materials or subassemblies. With just-in-time inventory, a company keeps on hand only those items needed for immediate use. In commenting on the use of temps, Susan Christopherson, a professor at the University of California at Los Angeles, has observed that "now we have just-in-time personnel management."[18] However, if the use of temporary workers offers the same benefits as just-in-time-inventory, it also presents the same challenges. There may not always be enough temps readily available, and there may be quality problems. However, these potential disadvantages must be viewed relative to Lehrer's model case: Similar labor market problems affect recruitment and retention of good permanent employees. An economic upturn that tightens the available supply of temps may also increase turnover among regular staff, especially if they have grown weary of "feast-or-famine" workloads. As will be shown, the solution—as with just-in-time goods inventory—lies in effective job analysis, workload planning, and communication.

Personnel Administration

Beyond recruitment costs, personnel administration of regular staff is becoming increasingly complex and expensive. Some of the increased complexity is due to changes in federal and state tax and employee benefit rules. For instance, the 1986 Consolidated Omnibus Budget Reconciliation Act (COBRA), requires employers of 20 or more people to offer continued health care coverage to terminated employees and to survivors, divorced spouses, and dependent children of employees. For the latter group, coverage can continue, and must be administered, up to three years. The COBRA requirements are considered an administrative nightmare for employers, especially those in high-turnover industries such as retail food and data processing.

In another development, a recent U.S. Supreme Court ruling permits states to require employers to grant female employees up to four months of personal leave following childbirth. Federal legislation is pending to require employers to provide up to 18 weeks of parental leave to both mothers and fathers and up to 26 weeks of medical leave.

Thus, every employee who is hired; every candidate who is not hired; every employee who quits, is laid off, or is fired (and his or her spouse, ex-spouse, and children) is, to the employer, a potential source of expensive litigation under increasingly comprehensive and complex rules and regulations.

Not all personnel administration problems are new, of course. Complaints about overtime, pay rates, and job descriptions and the conflicts that grow out of work in dead-end, repetitive jobs are classic opportunities for union organizers as well as for Equal Employment Opportunity (EEO) complainants and other litigation-minded workers. As will be discussed in Chapter 7, which deals with legal aspects of alternative employment strategies, employment of temporaries does not automatically insulate an employer from these concerns. But legislation such as COBRA combined with employer efforts to cut large parts of their work forces, have prompted some companies to turn to temporary arrangements as a cost-effective alternative to the entanglements of traditional employment relationships.

Productivity

Direct and indirect personnel costs are, like other business costs, only inputs. Economic analysis of staffing alternatives is meaningless without some measure of relative quantitative and qualitative output, that is, productivity. Hewlett-Packard Co. of Palo Alto, California, employs some 140 contract professionals at its computer divisions. After costs of employee benefits are factored in, their hourly rates are about 20 percent higher than those of regular staff. According to Samuel Prather, manager of software engineering for the company's information technology group, "It's worth that 20 percent if you're looking to hire people quickly and who are already experienced; you don't have to train them, and that saves you money."[19]

Conversely, if the temps hired in Lehrer's hypothetical case proved to be less productive than the employees they replaced, there would be a quite different outcome.

The Quality Dimension

The performance of THS employees, short-term hires, and on-call staff appears to at least equal that of permanent staff in quality. The fact that temporaries are being engaged much more frequently, and at professional and technical levels, is evidence of this, especially given the much-heralded emergence of quality improvement and technical excellence as keys to the survival of American business.

Another indicator of the quality level of temporary employees is that, according to industry sources, about 50 to 75 percent of active THS employees can expect to be offered permanent employment by clients to whom they are assigned (although only 20 percent accept). Members of on-call pools (except for special cases such as retiree pools) frequently have standing offers of full-time employment from their employers.

One of the main reasons for employer satisfaction with the productivity of temporary workers lies in the focused nature of the temporary employment transaction; the employee is called in to meet specific needs within a specific time period. A supervisor in a large public accounting firm comments that temporaries offer "about 20 percent more productivity just from the standpoint that they are here to get a specific job done in a specific time frame." As one THS firm manager put it,

> Permanent employees can get kind of lax; the temp is always on the line. Our people go in to produce work. They don't know anybody, they don't know the company's history or who's doing what. There's less gossip, less office politics, and they're not trying to find out whom to cultivate to further their careers in the company.

Temp agency managers, in-house pool administrators, and the clients they serve agree that because temps are paid by the hour, and at a relatively high rate, the expectation that an hour's pay will be matched with an hour's work is more obvious to both parties. When a contract employee whose services are billed at $15 per hour for word processing, or $50 per hour for programming, disappears from the office for a time or is found engaged in some personal pursuit, it will likely get the supervisor's attention. The same diversion of a regular employee, even though his or her total wage and benefit costs might equal the contractor's hourly rate, often goes unquestioned. As managers and management experts are all too well aware—borderline performance may be tolerated grudgingly by supervisors who have neither the time, training, nor general disposition to deal with it in the context of a long-term relationship.

Increasing satisfaction with the performance of temporary workers is due in large part to increased professionalism in recruiting and screening by both THS firms and job shops. It is also due to computer technology that permits firms to inventory their workers' skills and experience and to match them to client needs on very short notice.

Training programs such as those conducted by Manpower Inc., and other large THS firms are likewise intended to ensure that THS employees are fully qualified when they report for an assignment. According to Cherlyn Davis, senior human resources representative at Burroughs Corp., these screening and testing programs are effective. She and others find that well-selected temps come to the job better qualified than applicants who may show up at the company's own personnel office, and they adapt to the new job with little orientation. [20]

Specialization plays a role as well. Increasing numbers of job shops and THS firms recruit individuals who have, for example, bilingual skills or technical skills in such areas as software design, law, and accounting. Recruiters who specialize in particular industries, for example, stock market analysts who follow only one industry, are typically better able to find the best performers than are generalist corporate recruiters.

However, BNA found that one of our fastest growing industries—health care—is backing away from use of temporary nurse registries. According to a 1984 survey conducted by the American Hospital Association (AHA), 22 percent of health care institutions were using the registries, down from 27 percent in 1983. Both AHA officials and union officials in the industry indicated that "continuity of care" was an issue. Health care institutions remain among the most intensive users of nonpermanent workers, however, and in some cases—especially those in which internal union pressure is involved—they have developed their own in-house temp pools to supplant the registry nurse system.

In general, BNA and others have found that the key quality issue is whether or not the work itself and the work environment lend themselves to temporary employment arrangements. The concern is not with the inherent capabilities of temporary workers. For example, a union organizer explained to BNA that registry nurses are a big issue with hospital nursing staffs because "they don't want to keep telling different temporary employees where supplies are located, night after night."[21]

The Quantity Dimension

Temporary workers spend more time on the job than permanent workers, but the differential is usually understated in traditional economic analyses such as those of Lehrer and the Chamber of Commerce discussed earlier. Traditional analysis limits "time not worked" to vacation, holidays, paid personal leave, and sick leave. In reality, casual tardiness and quitting early, stretched coffee and lunch breaks, and time spent on personal phone calls, other personal pursuits, and interoffice gossip and politics must be added to those more formal factors.

Finally, the expertise that skilled temporaries bring to the task increases both the quantity and quality of their output. At a number of locations of Johnson and Johnson Products, the company contracts with job shops for technical personnel such as drafters and programmers. Management information systems specialists have proved helpful in special assignments such as installation and start-up of new computer systems. A company spokesman explains:

> We have found consultants who are familiar with the system and experienced at helping our people get oriented to it. When the assignment is temporary, it makes little sense to try to hire a regular employee to bring our employees up to speed in that situation. It's easier to get someone in who knows that system, let them do it for three months, and then off they go.

Job Protection for Regular Employees

Many companies are increasing their use of temporary employees to minimize the need for reductions in permanent staff.

This is sometimes called the "ring-and-core" approach: the core of permanent employees is both functionally supported and insulated from layoffs by a ring of relatively expendable temporaries. The temps move in and out of the work force as required by business volume, and it is understood that they will be terminated before permanent workers. Apple Computer, for example, laid off 20 percent of its regular work force in 1986 and now hires temporaries for 5 to 10 percent of the remaining jobs. Michael Ahern, manager of staffing, explains, "If we bring someone on board full time, there is an implied obligation that the job won't disappear."[22]

Johnson and Johnson Products, too, trimmed its staff in recent years and is anxious to avoid further layoffs. Says a spokesman, "If you aren't sure whether you will need six or seven people in a section, it is better to go ahead and staff for six and budget for additional temporary help if you need it."

Mayall and Nelson expressed the problem more broadly:

> Maintaining [permanent] attachment is expensive, especially if demand and related workload fluctuate over time. As a worker continues in employment, the employer assumes contractual, legal and moral responsibilities to provide various levels of job security. The longer an employee's tenure, the more difficult it tends to be for the employer to be rid of responsibility if either need for or satisfaction with the employee diminishes.[23]

BNA found that 14 percent of survey respondents using THS temps, 8 percent using short-term hires, and 20 percent using on-call workers cited protection of core workers as a reason. In some cases, employers who opt to hire temporaries are seeking to reduce the likelihood of EEO discrimination charges growing out of reductions in force. In addition, employers are increasingly concerned about private lawsuits for unust dismissal. Courts in several states have awarded large damage settlements to terminated employees in some such cases, finding that implied contracts existed between employer and employee. As will be shown in Chapter 7, legal authorities agree that employees whose jobs are explicitly temporary are less likely to claim successfully that they have an implied contract for indefinite employment.

There are other reasons for using temporaries to stabilize the work environment of permanent employees. Layoffs frighten and sap the morale of the survivors. The watchword becomes "Who's next?" Rather than wait to find out, survivors—often the top performers management is counting on to operate a much tighter ship—begin making their own exits via job or career changes.

Temporary Staffing Decisions and Their Implementation

Thus far, case histories, survey data, anecdotal information, and the views of various experts have been presented to outline the circumstances under which employers use temporary staffing. We will now discuss factors that play a key role in determining the most effective way to use temporary staffing: (a) THS versus the in-house pool, (b) policy considerations, and (c) strategies for integration and control.

THS Firms Versus the On-Call Pool

These options are not mutually exclusive. Some firms both engage temps and administer their own on-call worker pools; some rely exclusively on THS firms and job shops. However, some companies, for instance, Bank of America and Firemans Fund Insurance Company, have made or are making the transition to exclusive reliance on their on-call workers to meet temporary staffing needs. Bankers Life Company of Hartford, Connecticut, reported that it saved $10,000 in THS fees in the first year of an on-call pool operation established in 1979.

The issue is not whether an in-house system is inherently better or worse than a third-party approach to temporary staffing needs. What is critical is that management properly identify and treat all the decision variables that apply to its unique situation. The company that attempts to establish an in-house pool to minimize temporary staffing costs vis-à-vis using THS firms and job shops is, in effect, establishing a new "profit center." The decision should therefore be based on the same sort of analysis as would a decision to establish a new profit center in the company's normal business operations.

There are several key variables to weigh in deciding whether to develop an in-house pool or use THS and job-shop personnel for temporary assignments. Because Bank of America's decision to switch from a THS to an in-house approach was based on a detailed analysis of relevant variables, the discussion that follows will frequently use its experience as a reference point to which other companies can compare their own situations. Key variables in weighing the merits of contracted temporary services versus those of internal temp arrangements are discussed in the following sections.

Developing and Maintaining an In-House Temp Roster

Assuming equal work quality and basic wage rates, will the net cost of operating and maintaining the in-house pool be more or less than the service fee charged by a THS firm or job shop? In making comparisons, it is important to keep in mind that an on-call worker is under "continuous recruitment," whereas, by definition, someone disposed to "temping" seeks the freedom to say with relative impunity, "No thanks, I have other plans this month." This orientation presents dilemmas for the in-house pool administrator. If, for example, a pool member can work only the first month of a two-month assignment, should the administrator confirm that arrangement and seek another pool member for the second month, or gamble on finding someone who can work both months? Whatever decision the administrator makes, it will be time-consuming: NATS officials estimate that an average of 6, and as many as 10 phone calls are typically required to locate a temp who is ready and willing to accept a given assignment.

The employer seeking to recruit for an in-house pool such as Bank of America's, where the workers do not have previous ties to the company, will find that the resources of THS firms that served it as a client will work against it as a competitor. For example, the employer must assess how and whether it can compete with THS firms with regard to employee benefits. Several large THS firms offer temporaries benefits such as paid holidays and vacation, credit union services, group life and health insurance, sign-up bonuses of $100, bonuses for referring other temps, and longevity bonuses. These benefits are contingent on the employee's working a set number of hours for the THS firm.

Typically, an employee must have worked 1,200 hours during the previous 12 months to receive holiday pay from the THS firm and 1,500 hours to receive 1 week's vacation pay. A THS temp who works 1,800 hours per year may receive 2 weeks' paid vacation. Some job shops provide similar benefits, and an even greater number permit active registrants to purchase their own life and health insurance at group rates. There are other incentives for temps to maintain ties to THS firms. Companies such as Manpower Inc., allow their temps to come to the office on their own time and improve job skills through the Skillware program. Some THS firms subsidize outside training.

Despite its lack of employee benefits for on-call workers, Bank of America competes successfully with THS firms because (a) local values and life-styles generate a relatively large pool of suitable applicants, and (b) the bank's high temporary-to-permanent conversion rate, its no-layoff policy, and the relatively stable working environment it can offer across multiple locations provide incentives that THS firms often cannot. Bank of America concedes that a program such as the one it offers might well prove unsuccessful in other circumstances. Employers seeking to set up an in-house pool should investigate the relevant forces at work in their own labor markets and assess whether they can deal with them—and at what cost.

Unemployment Compensation Costs

What will be the impact on the employer's unemployment compensation premiums of the hire-and-layoff cycle inherent in on-call pool operations? The unemployment compensation law in most states requires that a temporary employee be removed from active status through prompt notification by the employer when work is not available. If the employee remains on active status (available for work) with no work from the employer, he or she accrues time toward eligibility for unemployment compensation. Bank of America has had only six unemployment compensation claims filed against its account from among the 300 employees it has brought into the on-call pool. Addie Johnson attributes this low claims experience to "administrative quick thinking" by her coordinators in monitoring and matching worker availability to management needs.

Administration

Some of the administrative issues that should be addressed in weighing the relative merits of an in-house temp pool include questions of what the manpower, materials, and systems costs of establishing and maintaining the in-house temp pool roster will be and what the cost will be of adding—then removing—a worker from active payroll with each assignment. For all its careful planning, Bank of America found that it underestimated the administrative cost of operating its in-house pool.

Payroll

Most temporaries expect to be paid weekly. "It's part of their behavior profile," comments B of A's Johnson. Because the bank's payroll system was programmed for bimonthly pay periods, she bought a packaged payroll system from Bank of America's Business Systems Division to provide weekly pay for the on-call temps. Employers should consider whether their current payroll and benefits accounting system can easily accommodate on-call arrangements. If they cannot, will special pay codes and other systems and procedures modifications be necessary? Without such modifications, for example, would temps be counted as eligible for the employee benefits restricted to permanent employees, or would they show up on EEO reports and internal employee counts intended to reflect only regular staff? If modification to existing systems is not cost-effective, what will be the cost of a packaged program?

Federal law requires that when an employee has worked 1,000 hours in a year, he or she must be credited with a year's service toward certain benefit plans the employer may have established. Once an in-house temporary has begun work, who will track the hours to determine when he or she is approaching the 1,000-hour threshold? Here again, Bank of America has the resources to develop such a tracking system as well as the volume of business to make it cost-effective. Other companies may not. If some pro-rata benefits are provided to in-house temps, a system must be developed to administer them.

With a THS arrangement, in contrast, these problems fall to the THS firm as the legal employer of the temporary workers. The THS firm is just one more name on the client's vendor list, and one check per month is written for temporary services. The client's computer is not tied up processing paychecks, complex deductions, withholding and W-2 forms, and related reports. Remittance of payroll taxes to state and local authorities is likewise not a concern to the client.

Another issue is that of providing continuing guidance in legal and tax matters to an employer with on-call workers. Bank of America's Johnson cites these issues, along with administrative costs, as the most critical for employers to watch out for. She indicates that she relies on B of A's legal and tax staff for guidance in such areas as employee selection, nondiscrimination in assignments, and pay and benefits practices.

Bank of America had most of the necessary resources on hand for launching and maintaining a successful on-call program. Johnson concedes that although she had to do a great deal of work to put the program together, she "was surrounded by the resources [she] needed." These included sophisticated computer systems and expertise, a compensation department to help design a competitive pay program, expert tax and labor counsel, and a human resources staff that has enjoyed the new experience of managing the in-house program. Although it is not suggested that a company must be staffed and financed to the degree that Bank of America is before an on-call worker pool can be successful, the need for such administrative resources must certainly be taken into account in the planning process.

Policy Considerations

Avoiding Use of Temporaries to Fill Permanent Positions

Employers must address a number of human resource policy issues in employing or engaging temporary workers. The key policy consideration is to define what constitutes temporary work. As discussed earlier, legal authorities question whether a company can disclaim an employment relationship with THS workers engaged for lengthy or indefinite periods. Regardless of the legal issues in any such circumstance, there may well be negative reactions from permanent employees. One THS word processor who has worked continuously for 10 months as a replacement for a laid-off employee at a Maryland company recounts that as she walked through the company cafeteria, a regular employee commented loudly to her co-workers, "What's *she* still doing here? I thought she was temporary."

When "permanent temps" are staffed from an on-call pool, problems can come from the temps themselves. Several years ago, The Standard Oil Company began assigning its on-call pool employees to more or less continuous work because of a hiring freeze. Although they were working 40-hour weeks side by side with regular clerical workers, the pool workers received no employee benefits. As any practical distinction between them and the regular employees with whom they worked disappeared, the disparity in benefits eligibility became an increasingly sore point—so much so that it became a major issue in a union organizing drive conducted by 9to5, National Association of Working Women. Although they abandoned the organizing drive, the 9to5 pressure forced Standard Oil to begin extending fringe benefits to the temps in the on-call pool.

Later chapters will explore alternative staffing arrangements, such as employee leasing and individual contract arrangements, that may better meet management's concerns about increasing regular staff in times of uncertainty.

Other Policy Considerations

One question that management may wish to address before bringing temporary workers on board is, if an in-house approach is taken, are current personnel policies compatible with the philosophy and operation of an on-call arrangement? For example, could the on-call workers be given the same orientation packets and employee handbooks that are given to regular workers, or will a separate packet have to be established for them to reflect separate policies?

Other questions that may arise concern such issues as nepotism policy, exit interviews, physical examinations, or drug testing. Should in-house temps be allowed to bid for permanent job vacancies? If so, shouldn't inactive pool employees—not just those on the job at the time—be kept informed of permanent vacancies? How will this be accomplished? If a temp is hired as a permanent employee, should his or her temp service be counted toward eligibility for certain benefit plans? Some companies have policies requiring special approvals for "rehiring" a former employee. Even the normal hiring process involves personnel requisitions and action forms requiring lengthy processing and several levels of management approval, especially in today's lean staffing environment. How many of these policies and procedures will need to be rewritten and redesigned to fit the special nature of the on-call employment relationship?

Some of these potential problem areas must also be dealt with when the employer uses THS firms and job shops—especially when long-term assignments of individual employees are involved. But the issues are much more immediate in terms of costs, potential legal consequences, and human resource management implications when there is a direct employer-employee relationship.

Integration and Control

Integration

There are several steps an employer can take to integrate temporary workers smoothly into both the task and the social environment.

1. Learn to view the use of temporaries as a strategic tool rather than a response to a crisis. To the extent possible, management should plan and budget for temporary workers on a systematic basis. Research has confirmed the increased use of temporary workers by companies "on a planned basis, rather than as an expedient for dealing with an unforeseen situation."[24] Regular staff should be informed as to why and how the temporaries are to be used. Few events are more disconcerting to employees than to arrive at work to find strangers working in their or their co-workers' "territory."

2. Think through the work to be done in each case. A sense of purpose can be reinforced by applying the unity-of-command principle that is normally applied to permanent employees: that each employee should be responsible to one, and only one, supervisor. That person should be clearly identified. Too often, temporary workers are considered "utility people" who can and should respond to direction from anyone needing assistance. At Johnson and Johnson Products, each new temp—whether from a THS firm or the on-call pool—is assigned to an experienced employee holding a similar job for a one-on-one briefing.

3. Provide temporary workers the same orientation as permanent employees with respect to rules, regulations, and administrative procedures. Management tends to recognize the need for basic orientation with regard to regular staff, but overlook it with respect to temporaries. New employees need to know where to make copies, the location of washrooms and cafeterias, how to requisition supplies, correspondence formats, and VIP names. Even dialing the telephone can be mystifying to an employee unfamiliar with a given company's tie-line system and branch-access codes. Temps also must be aware of behavior constraints such as dress codes and smoking rules. Some companies have employee handbooks designed especially for temporary workers. (Exhibit 2.3 is an excerpt from one such handbook.)

4. Explain the specifics of the task to the worker. The supervisor should explain what is to be done or delegate an experienced employee to do so. Any such delegation should be made in advance so that the employee who is to lay out the work for the temp can prepare the necessary materials

Exhibit 2.3

OMARK INDUSTRIES
SPORTING EQUIPMENT DIVISION
LEWISTON, IDAHO, OPERATIONS

(The following was excerpted from the employee handbook presented to on-call employees.)

Welcome to the Lewiston Operations of the Sporting Equipment Division of Omark Industries. We're happy to have you with us as an Extraboard employee.

Before beginning your first job assignment, there are some things you should know about the company, some rules and regulations which apply to all of us, and some which apply specifically to Extraboard people.

The Extraboard is a group of people who have no specific job or department assignment. They are subject to call-in to work in any department in order to fill in for regular employees who are on vacation or leave of absence, or to augment the work force during peak production periods.

As an Extraboard person you are not guaranteed a minimum number of hours of work, nor can you expect to work throughout the year.

Extraboard employees receive no health and welfare benefits, except those mandated by law. These include social security, industrial insurance, and unemployment insurance. You will receive pay increases, commensurate with the number of hours you work in a job classification. Your starting rate of pay is the entry level amount for the classification in which you are working. Increases are given after 520 hours, 1040 hours, and 2080 hours of work in each classification.

There is no guarantee of employment in the regular work force for Extraboard employees. As a matter of fact, very few Extraboard people can ever expect to become part of the regular employee group. If openings do occur, certainly Extraboard people will be considered to fill them. However, selection will be made on the basis of skill and ability and not on the length of time spent working on the Extraboard.

Extraboard employees do not receive regular job evaluations. However, there is an Extraboard Evaluation form which is filled out periodically by the various supervisors for whom you will be assigned to work. Negative reports could result in the termination of your employment. More minor problems will require that you be counseled by a representative of the Personnel Department. Repeated difficulties will certainly result in your termination.

As an Extraboard employee you may decline to work on a specific shift or on certain days of the week. However, once you have established the shift and days you are available to work you must be prepared to work in any department. You will be expected to be by your phone at the following times on the days you have agreed to work:

Monday through Thursday

Shift	Call Hours
Days:	
6:00 a.m.–4.30 p.m.	5:30 a.m.–6:30 a.m.
Swing:	
4:30 p.m.–3:00 a.m.	4:00 p.m.–5:00 p.m.

Friday through Sunday

Weekends:	
6:00 a.m.–6:00 p.m.	5:30 a.m.–6:30 a.m.
6:00 p.m.–6:00 a.m.	5:30 p.m.–6:30 p.m.

Failure to respond to a call two days in a row will result in termination. If you know you will be unavailable for a specific period of time because of illness or personal business, you must call the Personnel Office in advance so your name can be removed from the call list for those days.

Source: The Bureau of National Affairs, Inc., *The Changing Workplace: New Directions in Staffing and Scheduling*. Special Report (Washington, D.C.: BNA, 1986), 111.

or make up written instructions. On occasion, office temporaries reporting to a new assignment find that their supervisor is in an early meeting or that no one has been assigned to outline the task. The problem is compounded when the supervisor returns, discovers the temporary sitting at a desk, and calls in a busy regular employee: "I forgot we have a temp in this week to fill in for Jane. Show her what to do, will you?" As temporary workers are well aware, the focus of the regular employees' displeasure in such cases is often directed at them.

Control

A flexible approach to staffing should not be confused with a casual approach to staffing. The relative ease with which temporary workers move in and out of the workplace can encourage inefficiencies and even abuse of the system by the managers who hire them. Systematic planning facilitates controls to prevent such problems. There are three basic types of management controls—precontrol, concurrent control, and feedback control. With respect to temporary staffing, control may be planned and implemented in a number of ways. The following are just a few examples.

Precontrol. When temporary staff salaries are made a budget line item for a department, they can be monitored like any other line item. In addition, when temporary employees are sought for an unusually long period of time, management may wish to require that personnel requisitions be completed and the situation explained, regardless of budgeted funds available. Generally, agreements and contacts with THS firms, job shops, and freelancers should be made through or by a central source such as the personnel department. This will avoid duplication of effort and the possibility of inadvertent violation of labor laws and regulations such as the Employee Retirement Income Security Act of 1974 (ERISA) reporting requirements or reporting requirements for miscellaneous income under Internal Revenue Service (IRS) rules. It also provides a focal point for quality control.

In the case of on-call worker pools and short-term hires, precontrol is best exercised in the selection process, just as it is with regular staff. When THS firm or job-shop employees are involved, management should make clear that it will not pay for time worked by an employee who does not meet the standards expected and will not continue to do business with a supplier that seems not to understand its work standards.

To limit costs and obtain overall favorable terms, management should consider soliciting competitive bids and proposals from THS firms and technical service job shops when high-volume use is anticipated. This has the added advantage of requiring these firms to present for formal comparison their quality control processes, such as training and evaluation of employees, and to present the qualifications of their own management teams. (See Appendix A, where a bulletin from the National Technical Services Association (NTSA) on recommended practice for purchasing contract technical services is reprinted.) Although it would normally be coordinated by the human resources department, hiring managers should be very much a part of the vendor evaluation process.

As a further element of precontrol, any formal agreement entered into with a THS firm, job shop, or individual should be reviewed and approved by the employer's legal counsel. It is especially important that such agreements establish clearly that the third party is the worker's employer, or in the case of a freelancer, that the individual is truly a self-employed, independent contractor. (See Appendices B and C, where standard form agreements recommended by the National Technical Services Association are reprinted.)

Concurrent Control. Supervisors should closely monitor the output of new temporary workers, and even that of their "regular temps" when they are in new assignments. Because there is a greater tendency for instructions to temporaries to be made with less forethought and structure (i.e., relatively weak precontrol), there is a greater chance of misunderstanding. Written instructions and a single point of contact for the temp who has any doubt about what to do in a given circumstance will facilitate the process.

Where job shoppers are hired for more creative work such as design, this process may take some discussion with the employee. Even in those cases, however, there are usually specifications and parameters as to time, cost, and materials that, if clearly communicated to the employee, can make it easier to evaluate progress. Formal procedures should be established for evaluation of temporary workers in each assignment.

A final area of concurrent control involves legal issues. There is a particular concern here with respect to on-call employees. Bank of America's Johnson sums it up: "If they're your employees, you're liable." Without some point of control, in-house temps may be assigned by department managers with little or no thought given to compliance with nondiscrimination statutes. "They're only temps," the reasoning goes. The problem is compounded because temporary workers are often excluded from the employer's EEO-oriented work force analyses. Because they have the same right to bring legal action against the employer as do permanent workers, it is important that their deployment—including their selection for permanent jobs—be monitored for patterns and practices adverse to protected groups.

Feedback Control. It is not uncommon for a relatively unproductive temporary worker to be assigned to a number of departments in the same organization in succession. This occurs when no one tracks the employee's performance and disenchanted supervisors simply make a mental note not to request that person's services again. Generally, written performance appraisals should be completed on temporary workers. The frequency of such appraisals with respect to one particular worker may vary; it may be unnecessary and burdensome to complete a performance appraisal form at the conclusion of each brief assignment of a long-time regular temp who works in one department.

Temporary worker performance data should go to the person responsible for administering the on-call pool or maintaining liaison with third parties. Companies such as Johnson and Johnson Products regularly call in representatives of the THS firms they engage to review the quality of service being provided. A spokesman explains, "They should be earning their fee by providing us quality employees, so we encourage our department managers to let us know when that is not the case."

Future Directions in Temporary Staffing

The forces that gave rise to increased use of temporary workers as an alternative to permanent employment are generally expected to remain with us, if not accelerate. These forces include the shift from production of goods to processing of information and other service industries; employer reluctance to add permanent staff in the face of possible business downturns; increased technology that both requires special expertise and facilitates its deployment; and the availability of capable individuals who either must, or prefer to, enter the temporary labor market. As summarized by Gannon:

> The number of temporary workers will probably increase substantially, because the industry provides job opportunities that do not require a full-time commitment and, at the same time, helps businesses to solve many staffing problems, such as the need for additional workers during busy periods. [25]

There is, too, a "learning curve" effect in the growing use of temporary workers. As employers learn how to plan for, select, integrate, and productively control temporary staff as an ongoing, rather than a "fire-fighting" strategy, the practice will become more accepted generally in management circles.

If there is to be a major impediment to use of temporary staff, it may come in the form of litigation or legislation, or both. As will be discussed in Chapter 6, legal experts are concerned about companies' use of the same THS employees for indefinite periods. Such a practice may raise a question as to whether the THS client, and not the THS firm, is the true employer for legal purposes. The practice seems to be growing in popularity. Granrose and Applebaum found that as many as 80 percent of requests received by some THS firms are for long-term assignments.[26]

As noted by Carey and Hazelbaker, THS temps accounted for less than one percent of total wage and salary employment in nonagricultural establishments in December 1985.[27] It is apparent from the case histories presented, however, that temporary workers play a useful role for both management, regular employees, and many of the temporary workers themselves. It may be up to management and the THS industry to determine whether the practice continues to flourish or is hampered by adverse legislation and regulatory findings based on real or perceived abuses.

Notes

1. The Bureau of National Affairs, Inc., *The Changing Workplace: New Directions in Staffing and Scheduling*. Special Report (Washington, D.C.: BNA, 1986).
2. W.W. Macauley, "Developing Trends in the Temporary Services Industry," *Personnel Administrator*, January 1986, 61.
3. M.L. Carey and K.L. Hazelbaker, "Employment Growth in the Temporary Help Industry," *Monthly Labor Review*, April 1986, 37–43.
4. S. Silver, "Why You Might Consider Trying Contract Engineering," *National Business Employment Weekly*, 15 September 1985, 5.
5. The Bureau of National Affairs, Inc., *Flexible Staffing*. Exclusive Results of Survey on U.S. Firms' Use of Non-Regular Employees. Special Supplement to *BNA's Employee Relations Weekly*, 8 September 1986.
6. D. Mayall and K. Nelson, *The Temporary Help Supply Service and the Temporary Labor Market*. Office of Research and Development Employment and Training Administration, U.S. Department of Labor, Research Development Grant 21-49-81-14 (Salt Lake City: Olympus Research Corp., 1982), 36.
7. C. Trost, "Labor Shortages in Entry Level Jobs Force Companies to Make Adjustments," *The Wall Street Journal*, 3 June 1986, 1.
8. Mayall and Nelson, *Temporary Help Supply Service*, note 6, above, 36.
9. P. Rivers, "Skillware: Manpower's Training Door to the Future Gives Secretaries the Key," *The Secretary*, April 1986, 2.
10. S.K. Hamburg, *Manpower Temporary Services: Keeping Ahead of the Competition*. A case study for Work in America Institute's "Training for the New Technology" policy report (Scarsdale, N.Y.: Work in America Institute, Inc., 1986), 12.

11. BNA, *The Changing Workplace*, note 1, above, 30.
12. E. Carlson, "Longer Work Life?" *Modern Maturity*, June–July 1985, 8.
13. BNA, *The Changing Workplace*, note 1, above, 86.
14. C.A. Connelly, " 'Lease to Hire' Offers a Risk-Free Approach to DP Staffing," *Data Management*, June 1985, 45.
15. A. Strong, "Leased Gun for Hire," *Network World*, 28 July 1986, 26.
16. Mayall and Nelson, *Temporary Help Supply Service*, note 6, above, 60.
17. R.N. Lehrer, Ed., *White Collar Productivity*, McGraw-Hill Series in Industrial Engineering and Management Science (New York: McGraw-Hill, 1983).
18. BNA, *The Changing Workplace*, note 1, above, 6.
19. L. Reibstein, "More Companies Use Free-Lancers to Avoid Cost, Trauma of Layoffs," *The Wall Street Journal*, 18 April 1986, 22.
20. K. Ivers, "Working With a Can-Do Attitude," *Focus*, 14 August 1985, 2.
21. BNA, *The Changing Workplace*, note 1, above, 17.
22. M.A. Pollock and A. Bernstein, "The Disposable Employee Is Becoming a Fact of Corporate Life," *Business Week*, 15 December 1986, 56.
23. Mayall and Nelson, *Temporary Help Supply Service*, note 6, above, 28–29.
24. C. Granrose and E. Applebaum, "The Efficiency of Temporary Help and Part-Time Employment," *Personnel Administrator*, January 1986, 72.
25. M.J. Gannon, "Preferences of Temporary Workers: Time, Variety, and Flexibility," *Monthly Labor Review*, August 1984, 26.
26. C. Granrose and E. Applebaum, "The Efficiency of Temporary Help and Part-Time Employment," note 24, above.
27. M.L. Carey and K.L. Hazelbaker, "Employment Growth in the Temporary Help Industry," note 3, above.

3

Employee Leasing

As the term is most commonly used, *employee leasing* is a process whereby an employer terminates its employees and the workers are then hired by a third party—the employee leasing company—which leases them back to the original employer. As the employer of record, the leasing firm assumes, in theory, all normal employer functions and legal responsibilities. Such functions include hiring, firing, employee performance evaluation, payroll, day-to-day personnel administration and record keeping, employee benefits plan administration, and making legally required payments of income taxes withheld and workers' compensation and unemployment insurance premiums. Work direction of the employees is usually overseen by employees designated by the leasing company to be supervisors at the client's site. In most cases these individuals were supervisory employees of the client before their conversion to the leasing company payroll. Most leasing firms maintain a staff of field supervisors who periodically call on the client to monitor the service provided, conduct performance appraisals, deal with employee-related problems, and otherwise service the account.

The leasing company typically provides comprehensive employee benefits, and it may offer services such as a credit union and employee awards programs. Employee leasing organizations that offer this range of services are called *full-service* leasing firms. They stand in contrast to those which provide only a payroll and payroll-tax-paying service or limit their scope to pension plan tax advantaging for the benefit of client company owners. However, full-service firms may also include tax-advantaged pensions among their services. Employee leasing is sometimes called *staff leasing*, *contract staffing, employee contract services*, and *human resource leasing*. The terms *employee leasing* and *staff leasing* will be used interchangeably in this chapter.

Staff leasing firms differ from temporary help service companies and job shops in that they usually furnish permanent, rather than temporary, employees. In fact, some staff leasing firms will not accept clients in high-turnover industries such as restaurants. Because of the permanent status of leased workers, the employer is usually more involved in employee selection and evaluation than it would be in a typical THS or job-shop arrangement. In some cases, the working owner of the client firm may become an employee of the leasing firm.

Development and Growth of the Employee Leasing Industry

Employee leasing has been practiced for many years, notably by firms that provide truck drivers, plant security personnel, maintenance workers, and cafeteria workers. The significant developments that have occurred over the past decade, which are the focus of this chapter, are largely tied to three federal laws covering employee benefit plans.

The Employee Retirement Income Security Act of 1974 (ERISA)

Prior to ERISA, some employers used employee leasing firms to get around Internal Revenue Service regulations governing participation of rank-and-file workers in qualified pension plans. These regulations generally required employers to cover a significant proportion of rank-and-file workers in their pension plans and to make contributions on behalf of those workers comparable to those made on behalf of owners, executives, stockholders, and other highly compensated employees. By leasing employees, business owners were able to circumvent the regulations and establish relatively generous, "top-heavy" (sometimes called "top hat") pension plans for themselves and their highly paid staff.

ERISA was adopted to eliminate this and other perceived weaknesses in existing pension law. It required that if a leasing company and client company management had common control of rank-and-file workers, the client was the workers' employer for purposes of the nondiscrimination pension requirements.

A number of employee leasing firms continued to work with clients, particularly professional medical associations, to take advantage of perceived loopholes in ERISA. Several court cases ensued between the IRS and such associations. In 1980, Congress amended the Internal Revenue Code in an attempt to clarify the definition of professional associations and affiliated service groups. The 1980 amendments were criticized as poorly drawn, however, and they apparently added to the confusion.[1]

The Tax Equity and Fiscal Responsibility Act of 1982 (TEFRA)

Because of continued perceived abuses of federal pension regulations by physicians and others, as well as the vague language of the 1980 Tax Code amendment, Congress moved to resolve the employee leasing question as it related to benefit plans. It amended the law so that leased employees were considered the employees of the organization for which they provided services *unless* the recipient of the services provided them with a minimum level of pension benefits. The specific requirements were that the plan maintained by the leasing company

- be a money-purchase pension plan providing for a nonintegrated employer contribution equal to 7.5 percent of the employee's compensation;
- provide for immediate participation; and
- provide full and immediate vesting.[2]

Plans meeting these criteria were called "safe harbor" plans.

Although leasing firms already were being formed for other reasons, TEFRA was clearly responsible for the rapid growth of the industry following its passage. Virtually all of the leasing firms that sprang up served small businesses, with concentration in medical and related operations such as nursing homes. Articles on the staff leasing boom were common in the business and popular press. *Nation's Business* reported that the industry grew from 4,000 to 60,000 workers between October 1983 and October 1984.[3] By April 1985, *Fortune* reported that staff leasing employment was estimated to be about 75,000 with some 275 leasing firms in operation.[4] In their 1985 book, *Re-Inventing the Corporation*, Naisbitt and Aburdene stated,

> We are shifting from hired labor to contract labor, which
> is part of a larger trend of contracting out for a variety of services.

> Employee leasing . . . is enjoying a phenomenal boom. . . .
> We think that within a decade, as many as 10 million of us will
> be "leased" employees.[5]

The reputation of the industry was marred, however, when in March 1984, a large staff leasing firm, Paystaff, Inc., of Long Beach, California, went bankrupt. An investigation was launched by the IRS, the U.S. Department of Labor, and California authorities to locate more than $500,000 in back taxes and pension money.[6]

In late 1985, Omnistaff, Inc., one of the largest and most highly publicized leasing firms, also filed for bankruptcy. According to the attorney serving as the company's bankruptcy trustee, its total liabilities were $9 million, including $650,000 in bounced payroll checks, plus federal income and Social Security taxes, state unemployment taxes, and insurance premiums, including workers' compensation.[7] *Fortune* reported that some 75 leasing firms went out of business in 1985.[8]

The Tax Reform Act of 1986

The 1986 Tax Reform Act modified the TEFRA pension rules covering leased workers. The Act, which became effective January 1, 1987, increased the required contribution to leased employee pension plans from 7.5 percent to 10 percent, and it prohibits a company from excluding leased employees from its retirement plan if more than 20 percent of its employees are leased. It also requires that any employee of the leasing company client firm who earns $1,000 or more within a year must be included in the client's safe-harbor plan (a change from the former 1,000-hour rule). Legal and other experts—both within and outside the leasing industry—agree that the 1986 Act virtually eliminates the incentive for employers to use staff leasing as a tax shelter for top-heavy pension plans. Accordingly, leasing firms that specialized in safe-harbor leasing are either going out of business or joining the ranks of "commercial" leasing firms, that is, those that offer staff leasing services without the safe-harbor pension feature.

Case Histories

The case histories that follow describe a small sample of the practices of employee leasing firms today and the benefits perceived by their clients and employees. They illustrate important differences in both operating procedures and philosophy among staff leasing firms that, overall, provide similar services to similar clients.

Consolidated Employee Benefits Corporation (CEBCOR)

Consolidated Employee Benefits Corporation (CEBCOR) is an employee leasing firm headquartered in Chicago. It is one of the larger firms in the industry, with offices in Detroit, Dallas, Boston, and Los Angeles and 35 administrative employees. It leases about 400 employees to 50 client corporations and partnerships. CEBCOR clients represent a variety of industries such as manufacturing, construction, retail, consulting, and trade groups. Client staff complements range from 1 to 200 employees, representing all categories from unskilled laborers to professionals and managers. All but one of the owners of the client firms are CEBCOR employees; they are leased to the client companies, which, technically, have no employees. The work forces leased were previously employed by the clients; they were transferred to the CEBCOR payroll through the "fire-and-hire" process described earlier in this chapter. However, CEBCOR is negotiating with at least one potential client to provide start-up staffing. The company performs all recruiting and hiring functions for ongoing personnel needs of its clients, administers performance appraisals, and works with client and employee when on-the-job problems arise. It performs all payroll, employee benefits administration, record keeping, and other personnel administration tasks that normally fall to employers. When necessary, CEBCOR removes unsatisfactory employees and provides replacements. The client is responsible for day-to-day direction of the leased workers, gives input to employee performance reviews, and selects from among job candidates presented by CEBCOR.

Like most commercial leasing firms, CEBCOR sees the effective demise of safe-harbor leasing as a stimulus, rather than a hindrance, to employee leasing. CEBCOR marketing vice president Keith Crossland points out that the company has gained many clients since passage of the 1986 Tax Reform Act because there is now "more thought of efficiency as opposed to trying to exclude certain employees from a pension plan." In fact, one of CEBCOR's clients is Bartex, Inc., a Dallas construction company that had been a client of the defunct Omnistaff, Inc., leasing organization.

Many of CEBCOR's clients are small businesses that sign up simply to eliminate the burden of government-required personnel paperwork. The key motivation of its clients, however—as evidenced by the CEBCOR name—is the leasing firm's ability to provide substantially better benefits to employees than they could obtain as individuals or as employees in small groups. CEBCOR has found that the monthly premium for an unmarried employee in a small group can range as high as $140 to $150 per month for coverage consisting of (a) medical insurance with a $500 deductible and 80-20 co-insurance up to the first $5,000 of coverage and (b) life insurance coverage of $5,000 to $10,000. Because of its greater purchasing power, CEBCOR provides the following single-employee coverage:

- medical insurance with a $150 deductible;
- dental coverage;
- prescription eyeglass coverage;
- prescription drug coverage; and
- $10,000 life insurance coverage.

CEBCOR reports proportionately similar savings for employees with dependent coverage. All coverages except vision care are provided through Mutual of Omaha. The company suggests that by saving the small employer $50 to $70 per month per employee while providing superior benefits coverage, "it's like giving the employee a raise while improving the client's cash flow." The company also provides employees a 401(k) deferred savings plan, in which they may participate at their discretion.

Vice president Crossland notes that most health insurers will not even talk to many small employers. In those cases, the employer often secures individual policies on its employees, which are even more expensive than small-group policies.

According to Crossland, leasing usually reduces clients' unemployment compensation premiums because CEBCOR's state unemployment compensation premiums tend to be lower than those of the small businesses they serve. The company attributes the low turnover in part to the benefits it provides. Employees who might otherwise have left a client will remain with it as CEBCOR employees because of the enhanced benefits. Crossland claims, too, that when an employee is terminated, the company's personnel staff is often able to place the individual with another client or provide outplacement assistance—something few small businesses are equipped to do.

CEBCOR normally requires an advance deposit from the client equal to gross wages for one pay period. It bills clients each pay period on the basis of actual, documented costs of employment of the workers assigned plus a fixed service fee per employee. Costs include wages, employee benefit contributions, FICA and withholding taxes, workers' compensation premiums, and other statutorily required payments. Unlike some staff leasing firms, CEBCOR does not routinely furnish its clients periodic, audited statements that it has made all required tax withholdings and other legally required payments, but it is planning to do so.

CEBCOR charges a flat service fee that generally ranges from $5 to $15 per employee per week, with higher-volume clients paying in the lower range. The client must pay CEBCOR's invoice on the day CEBCOR distributes paychecks to the employees. CEBCOR guarantees the fixed fee for the initial 12-month lease agreement; after that time it is subject to renegotiation. The client, however, may cancel the agreement at any time upon 30-days' notice.

The Mount Prospect Lawnmower Company, which sells and services lawn mowers and accessories in Arlington Heights, Illinois, is typical of CEBCOR's smaller clients. Owner-supervisor Bill Becker became interested in staff leasing after his bookkeeper left the company, requiring him to divert time from running the business to doing paperwork—a task for which he was not trained. In some instances, he did not have the payroll prepared on time, and his employees had to go without paychecks. Becker leased himself and his six employees to CEBCOR in May 1986 and is quite pleased with the results. He cites the relief from paperwork and other administrative chores as the most significant business benefit. For example, it is no longer necessary for him to pay an outside accountant to compute payroll taxes. Leasing also relieves him of the "end-of-the-quarter scramble" he previously experienced in calculating and remitting legally required tax withholdings and other payments on behalf of employees. He comments,

> Leasing has helped me budget better so I can avoid penalties and interest for untimely payments. I pay the leasing company a flat amount each week; I don't have to scramble every quarter to come up with that additional money to satisfy the government. Leasing has taken a tremendous burden off me.

He estimates that, after factoring for CEBCOR's service fee, staff leasing saves his business from $300 to $400 per month in personnel administration expenses alone. In addition, CEBCOR's unemployment insurance premium, which is passed through to the lawnmower company, is considerably lower than that previously paid by Becker.

Becker also finds that, through CEBCOR, he can offer more employee benefits at a lower cost than before. As a small employer, he had been unable to offer his employees dental, vision care, or prescription coverage. His staff now has all three coverages at what he describes as a very favorable rate obtained through CEBCOR's buying power. Becker reports that his staff members "love the benefits" they receive as CEBCOR employees. Two employees require regular prescription drugs that previously had cost them about $60 per month; with prescription coverage under the CEBCOR medical plan, the drugs cost them $2 per month.

Under the company's health insurance plan before leasing, the employee deductible was $200; it is now $100. The CEBCOR plan also provides outpatient coverage; the previous plan did not. For cost reasons, the company has no pension plan, nor did it have one prior to leasing the staff. Becker periodically solicits cost quotations for medical and workers' compensation insurance to be certain that CEBCOR's rates are competitive; thus far, he has found them to be quite favorable.

Staff Services, Inc.

Staff Services, Inc., is an employee leasing firm located in Virginia Beach, Virginia.[9] It has been in business since 1981 and supplies 200 workers—90 percent of them women—to 60 client firms nationwide. Client staff complements range from 1 to 15 employees. Like CEBCOR, Staff Services, Inc., has a diverse client base including retail operations, real estate and law firms, physical therapy and nursing services, and city and state governments. The company will employ working owners only if it employs all other workers of the client.

The company's owner and president, J. Andrew Butler, is a founder and past president of the National Staff Leasing Association, a Los Angeles-based industry association representing about 100 leasing firms. He is among those who welcome the industry's disassociation from tax sheltering. His firm previously offered both safe-harbor and commercial leasing, but terminated its pension plan after passage of the 1986 Tax Reform Act. He notes that because of safe harboring, "we were perceived as a device by which the wealthy could effectively disenfranchise employees of benefits. The market is much larger now because we don't have the pension costs."

As an employer, Staff Services, Inc., provides all recruiting, employment, payroll, personnel and benefits administration services, and employee services to its workers. Unlike CEBCOR, however, Butler maintains that the legal relationship between his firm and its clients is a "co-employer" relationship. To avoid potentially costly legal implications for itself and its clients, Staff Services, Inc., is revising its contracts to spell out the joint employer responsibilities of each party.

The company's contracts are for one year, and they can be cancelled by the client upon 30 days' notice. Staff Services, Inc., recently converted from a cost-plus-fixed-fee billing schedule to cost plus a percentage of gross wages. Butler is now considering individually negotiated fee schedules based on the client's volume and employee turnover.

Staff Services, Inc., employees receive hospitalization, medical, dental, and life insurance coverage. For the past four years, Butler has used Browning Insurance Group of Virginia Beach to design its group insurance packages. According to Robert Gentry, a broker with Browning, he can secure comprehensive, low-cost coverage at lower rates by pooling employees of the leasing firm's many small clients. He points out that in employee groups of fewer than 10, group insurance carriers base premium rates on the age and sex of group members. In larger groups, those are not rating factors. He cites an example of group insurance coverage for a 30-year-old employee in a typical group of fewer than 10: Health care coverage would cost $236.87 per month for such an individual. In a non-age-rated group of 50 to 60 workers, Gentry can secure the same coverage for $197 per month.[10]

When Blue Cross and Blue Shield raised premium rates to Staff Services, Inc., by 33 percent in October 1986, Gentry was able to shop for alternative coverage. Staff Services, Inc., now has a preferred provider hospitalization and medical plan in place of the Blue Cross-Blue Shield plan. Gentry is currently exploring flexible compensation plans under which employees may convert certain amounts of wages to nontaxable employee benefits. When plan changes are recommended by Gentry, Staff Services, Inc., clients are involved in the decision, and when the changes are approved, Gentry communicates them to the affected employees.

One Staff Services, Inc., client is Comprehensive Rehabilitation Services of Tidewater, Inc., a multitherapy practice. Susan Glaser, owner and president of the firm, is leased to the company as are all other staff members. They include physical therapists, occupational therapists, hand therapists, therapy assistants, and office staff. There are six full-time staff members, and the company is currently adding one part-time worker.

Comprehensive Rehabilitation Services started up with leased employees in July 1982. Glaser had 20 years of professional experience as an occupational hand therapist, but none in payroll, bookkeeping, or personnel administration. "I've always felt you should stick with the skill you've been trained in and let somebody else worry about these other things," she comments. In her case, the "somebody else" is Staff Leasing, Inc.

In addition to giving her more time for patient contact and for directing her professional staff, the leasing arrangement provides the employee benefits necessary to compete for skilled employees. She notes that experienced therapists "don't come cheap, and they want good benefits."

Glaser is also pleased with the fact that Staff Leasing, Inc., provides personnel manuals to the employees and is their point of contact for questions or complaints about personnel policy. "They cover them from A to Z," she says. She feels that this process strengthens her relationship with her staff, who regard her more as a professional colleague than an administrator. In recruiting, the leasing firm handles advertising and screening of candidates. "They only send me the cream of the applicants," says Glaser, "so I don't waste my professional time talking to five or six therapists for one position."

When Staff Services, Inc., terminated its pension plan following enactment of the 1986 Tax Reform Act, Glaser's staff were affected. However, she has discussed it with them and is considering alternate forms of compensation. She reports that, overall, elimination of the pension plan has not been a problem.

Primarily because staff leasing frees her from the paperwork burden of payroll and personnel administration, Glaser says she cannot imagine running a small business any other way. She concludes, "I'm a very devoted hand therapist, so I'll gladly give the headaches to Mr. Butler."

Patterns in Usage and Operation
of Employee Leasing

Data on the scope and usage of staff leasing are difficult to obtain. In its present form, the practice is relatively new; the industry is populated by small firms serving even smaller firms. Because of the major impact of the 1986 Tax Reform Act on leasing firms that were wholly or partially engaged in safe harboring, it is an industry in transition, if not turmoil. There are problems of definition as well. Is a contract security guard service an employee leasing company? And, given the differences in method of operation, could not THS firms be called employee leasing companies in terms of their basic function? In some cases, they are. Chapter 2, "Temporary Workers," cited cost analyses done by Lehrer with respect to use of THS employees; in his original material, he referred to THS employees as "leased workers."

Much of the aggregate data available on staff leasing comes from Arno & Associates, a Los Angeles-based consulting firm to the industry; the National Staff Leasing Association; and National Staff Network, a Van Nuys, California, organization representing many staff leasing firms. A Bureau of National Affairs, Inc. (BNA), special report on flexible staffing gave one of the first clear pictures of the scope and dimensions of the leasing phenomenon, and its findings will be drawn upon here.[11] The 1986 report prepared for the U.S. Small Business Administration by Young and Elliott, cited earlier in this chapter, was based on a survey of 14 leasing companies and 21 clients.[12] Of those firms, 20 had fewer than 100 workers each; the other had 500 or more workers. Because the sample sizes were small and nonrandom, Young and Elliot cautioned that the data cannot support generalizations about the leasing industry or its practices. Nevertheless, theirs was a methodical and revealing research study, and it will be referred to frequently here.

Another study of staff leasing was conducted by the U.S. Department of Health and Human Services (HHS) in 1986.[13] Although the report was based mostly on secondary research that relied heavily on leasing industry sources, it, too, will be cited here.

Geographic Distribution of Staff Leasing Companies

Young and Elliott's analysis of aggregate data revealed that, of the 300 employee leasing firms identified in Arno & Associates'

Directory of Employee Leasing Companies, 72, or 24 percent, were located in California. The six populous states of California, Texas, New York, Florida, Ohio, and Pennsylvania accounted for 157 leasing firms, or about half of the total. Ohio had only 14 leasing firms, and Pennsylvania 12; seven states had none.[14] Arno notes that leasing companies that have offices in several states are listed only under the state in which they have their headquarters. Nonetheless, employers in nonmetropolitan areas who are considering staff leasing may find a limited selection of suppliers from which to choose. Some leasing firms do not accept clients located more than a given distance from their offices.[15]

Profile of Industries Served by Staff Leasing Firms

The 21 leasing company clients surveyed by Young and Elliott had from 2 to 50 leased workers, with an average of 12. Of the clients served, 11 were either medical doctors or dentists, and the others represented a range of businesses and professions such as light manufacturing, law practice, retail stores, printing, and engineering consulting. Most of the clients had been leasing employees for from one to five years.[16] Although most leasing company clients are small firms, there are indications that some large employers are considering staff leasing for some parts of their operations. For example, one large company with a nationwide chain of franchised retail outlets is exploring employee leasing as a service to its independent franchisees. The company describes their franchises as "mom and pop" stores that are similar to many other small firms. The company anticipates that a staff leasing arrangement might benefit the franchisees most by relieving them of recruiting and personnel paperwork in a high-turnover labor environment. The company indicates that because each franchisee is an independent contractor, there may be legal difficulties in structuring such an arrangement. The issue is currently under study by the company's counsel.

Categories of Leased Employees

Table 3.1 shows the distribution by general occupational category of the 254 leased workers serving the 21 client firms surveyed by Young and Elliott. The professional and technical and clerical categories each accounted for 88 employees, or 69.2 percent of the total collectively. Because of the heavy representation of medical

Table 3.1

NUMBER OF LEASED EMPLOYEES REPRESENTED BY CLIENT SAMPLE BY OCCUPATION

Occupational Category	No. of Employees in Study	Percentage of Total
Professional and Technical	88	35%
Managers and Administrative	3	1
Sales	5	2
Clerical	88	35
Operatives	13	5
Laborers	24	9
Craftworkers	26	10
Service Workers	7	3
	254	100%

Source: Office of Advocacy, U.S. Small Business Administration. *Employee Leasing in Small Versus Large Businesses* (Washington, D.C.: SBA, 1986), 51.

firms in the sample, most of the employees were nurses, doctors' assistants, dentists' assistants, and clerical help.[17]

Union Representation

No data are available on the extent to which businesses employ people represented by collective bargaining agreements while simultaneously using leased employees in other job categories at the same facilities. Except for the traditional use of uniformed guard services, office cleaning services, and truck drivers, it appears that such a situation is quite rare. First, most leasing clients are small companies that are not likely to be union-organized. Second, they tend to be concentrated in service industries that are traditionally resistant to union inroads. Finally, staff leasing company owners and industry spokesmen indicate that few leasing firms will accept a client who proposes to fire its organized work force and lease them back as a union-busting tactic. Such schemes have run employers afoul of the National Labor Relations Act, and staff leasing firms of any sophistication are justifiably wary of them. Employees of leasing firms have the same legal rights to organize for collective bargaining as do other workers. However, there appears to have been no union organizing of staff leasing firms to date.

Billing Practices and Fee Structures

There are a number of variations in billing practices and fee structures for staff leasing. Some leasing firms require a new client to place "payroll on deposit," an amount equal to one or two months' net payroll. One staff leasing firm permits the client to pay the deposit in four monthly installments. Some require only a one-month deposit, but the client must provide payroll funds a month in advance. Other staff leasing firms negotiate the deposit individually with each client. Of seven leasing firms selected for in-depth interviews by Young and Elliott, five required deposits.[18] According to Carmen Arno, president of Arno & Associates, a more frequent practice is for the leasing company to charge a new client a "set-up fee" of $25 to $30 per employee, rather than require a deposit.

Companies such as CEBCOR charge their clients for documented costs directly associated with employment of the workers assigned (payroll, benefits, and payroll taxes), plus a fixed fee per person to cover the leasing firm's general and administrative expenses and profit. Other leasing companies calculate their fees as a percentage of payroll. Table 3.2 shows the method and amount of fees charged by the 14 leasing firms included in the Young and Elliot study. Eleven of those firms charged their clients for payroll plus 21 to 40 percent for benefits, administration, and services. Some of the leasing companies in the sample were safe-harbor companies, and thus could be expected to charge higher-than-average fees due to the 7.5 percent pension requirement.

Leasing firms may also charge separately for special services associated with turnover or for additional staffing requested by the client. One commercial leasing company in the Midwest charges clients a set-up fee of $15 for each employee added to a client's complement and $10 for each termination. It also charges if it must engage an employment agency to recruit for job vacancies. Young and Elliot found the same pattern in their research; 8 of their 14 survey firms charged for such services. In addition, some of the firms charged clients for THS firm fees when it was necessary to call on them to supply workers to replace vacationing leased workers.

Defining the Employment Relationship

This is the most critical factor to be assessed by any company considering staff leasing. It refers to the legal relationships among

Table 3.2

FEES CHARGED BY LEASING COMPANIES IN SURVEY

Service Fee (as % of payroll)	Number of Leasing Companies
21–30	5
31–40	6
41–50	1
confidential	2
Total	14

Gross Administrative Fee (as % of payroll)	Number of Leasing Companies
4–5	3
6–7	4
8–10	5
confidential	2
Total	14

Source: Office of Advocacy, U.S. Small Business Administration. *Employee Leasing in Small Versus Large Businesses* (Washington, D.C.: SBA, 1986), 35.

leasing company, client, and employee. Business owners who assume that they can transfer their legal responsibilities as employer to a third party simply by writing a contract that says so may be in for a rude and ruinous shock if a court or administrative agency determines that they have remained employers in fact, or are at least joint employers with the leasing firm.

The specific legal tests and their implications will be identified and analyzed in Chapter 7. Outlined in the following sections are four general approaches that employee leasing companies adopt, based on their view of the law and the related business risks.

The Conservative Approach

In 1986, Marvin Selter, chairman of the board of National Staff Network and president of Practice Service Corporation, a large staff leasing firm in Van Nuys, California, told a U.S. Senate subcommittee: *"Let me state immediately that most employee leasing companies are not doing business legitimately today in America."*[19]

Selter's view was that in order for a leasing company to survive a legal challenge to its claim of employer status (or conversely, for a client to survive a legal challenge to its claim of nonemployer status), the parties must operate in the following manner:

- The client's former employees are not terminated; they submit written resignations. Even though they are usually reassigned to the former employer's location, they must first go through a complete new-hire process with the leasing company, including verification of credentials.
- The leasing company must be at risk for payroll. It does not require the clients to make advance payroll deposits; it pays its employees with its own funds as would any other employer.
- The leasing firm provides universal employee benefits. The same benefit package is available to employees at all the employer's locations throughout the country. The client does not pick and choose the benefit package to be provided to the workers assigned to its job sites.
- The leasing company bills on a fee-for-service basis; it does not increase charges incrementally with each increase in FICA, workers' compensation premiums, or additional costs such as overtime earnings. It instead bills on a sliding scale. For example, the fee would be x for an employee who earns between p and q dollars biweekly; if the employee works overtime during a given payroll period or gets a salary increase, the fee is not increased if total pay remains below q dollars.

Selter concluded,

> In my definition of these three areas, no one can take issue with how we operate. Based on the labor codes and ERISA, we conform to every single statute. We and our clients have been audited by IRS and we have demonstrated beyond any doubt that those are our [the leasing company's] employees.

The Liberal Approach

Some employee leasing firms and their clients hold that the client may indeed exercise authority over personnel selection, rates of pay, bonuses, and job assignments, while passing off the concomitant accountability to the leasing firm as the "employer." CEB-COR believes, for example, that even though its clients may direct it to give bonuses and pay raises to employees, that fact does not suggest that the client is the true employer. "Our client is the corporation," a spokesman explains. "The corporation itself has no employees. In fact, if it's a corporation, even the owner, if he be the sole shareholder, is an employee." Apparently, the Department of Health and Human Services holds to this theory as well. It describes employee contract services as a technique that usually begins "when the original employer 'transfers' its work force to a leasing agency. However, the former employer retains its *full management control* of the work unit."[20]

The Joint Employer Approach

Many leasing companies are now persuaded that a typical staff leasing arrangement establishes a joint, or co-employer relationship between leasing firm and client. They point to the fact that, in determining liability for violations of labor law and nondiscrimination statutes, for example, courts and administrative agencies have found such relationships in a number of cases involving leased employees. Leasing companies and legal advisors with this orientation conclude that it is therefore best to acknowledge the joint employer relationship. Butler, of Staff Leasing, Inc., explains:

> It used to be that "co-employer" was a dirty word because most companies would discover that they were co-employers accidentally, as a part of some court action. You never want to find out that way that you're included in the liability. Co-employment is no more onerous than employment; it is simply that you have to know the ground rules. A growing segment of the industry is coming out with co-employment contracts where the duties and responsibilities of each co-employer are all clearly defined up front.

In such an arrangement, for example, the leasing firm would not go through the motions of appraising employee performance with "input" from the client; it might, instead, play a quasi-consulting role, providing client supervisors with procedural guides and training in performance appraisal, dealing with disciplinary problems, and so on. Rather than implement pay increases upon recommendations from the client, the leasing firm would conduct pay surveys and make recommendations to the client. In both cases, it would be clear that the client makes the decisions and has full employer accountability for any adverse consequences. Attorneys in the field and a number of staff leasing operators confirm this trend toward open and defined acknowledgment of a joint employer relationship.

Payrolling

In payrolling, the staff leasing firm puts the client's employees on its payroll only in the sense that their paychecks come from the leasing firm. The leasing firm is responsible only for timely and accurate processing of the payroll, remittance of payroll taxes, employee benefits administration, and related record keeping. Responsibility and accountability for all other personnel functions reside with the client, who remains the employer of the workers for all such purposes. The leasing firm performs none of the consultative services that are part of co-employer arrangements. Consultant Arno and others in the industry suggest that such companies are not staff leasing firms, but payroll services.

Employer Reasons for Staff Leasing

Industry data, the BNA findings, anecdotal accounts such as the case histories presented here, and other studies reveal consistent patterns in the reasons for which employers turn to staff leasing. In examining these patterns, however, it must be kept in mind that they are shifting. Safe-harbor tax advantaging, for example, is no longer an option for the great majority of employers who might otherwise benefit from staff leasing. As shown in Figure 3.1, the primary reasons for staff leasing among the 21 clients surveyed by Young and Elliott were to secure better employee benefits, reduce paperwork, and minimize the "hassles" attendant to the employer-employee relationship.

Improved employee benefits and relief from personnel paperwork are most frequently cited by representatives of the leasing industry when queried about their clients' motivations. Marvin Selter's comment to BNA is typical: "Forty percent of our new clients say they want out of the employee hassles—the DOL [Department of Labor] Census reports, the OSHA reports, the tax burdens, the paperwork."[21]

Advantages of Employee Leasing

Active leasing company clients surveyed by researchers and interviewed by the business and popular press are quite enthu-

Figure 3.1

REASONS FOR USING LEASING
(CLIENT INTERVIEWS)

REASON (MULTIPLE ANSWERS ALLOWED)

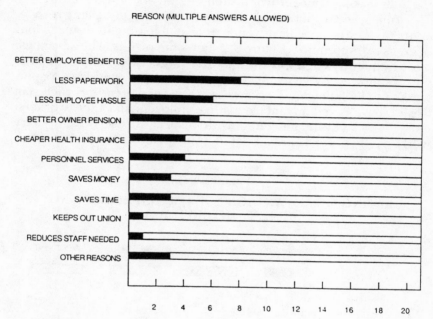

NUMBER OF CLIENT RESPONSES

Source: Office of Advocacy, U.S. Small Business Administration. *Employee Leasing in Small Versus Large Businesses* (Washington, D.C.: SBA, 1986), 40.

siastic about the advantages of staff leasing as an alternative employment strategy. Young and Elliott, for example, found that 20 of the 21 companies they interviewed were unable to cite a single drawback to their staff leasing arrangements. (One firm cited a small cash flow problem related to paying all staff salaries at one time.)[22] While there are no doubt companies that have tried staff leasing and found it disadvantageous, the industry claims that most of the former clients of the large leasing firms that went bankrupt are now clients of other leasing firms. One former Paystaff client is now with CEBCOR, and a former Omnistaff client, J.V.P. Co., of Hinckley, Ohio, was picked up by National Employer, Inc., a Cleveland-based staff leasing operation. As of July 1986, J.V.P's owner reported that he was quite pleased with the staff leasing concept. Given the business upheaval, personal trauma, and potential legal liabilities that a small business suffers when its staff leasing company goes bankrupt, it seems a valid endorsement of the staff leasing concept when such employers sign on anew.

Young and Elliot asked their leasing company client respondents to rate the specific advantages of staff leasing in terms of four degrees of importance. Figure 3.2 shows the results. The advantage most frequently cited as very important was "more employee benefits," followed by "cheaper employee benefits" and "less paperwork."[23] The following sections discuss several areas in which staff leasing has proved advantageous to employers and their workers. As with the advantages cited with respect to use of temporary workers, they are closely related. The pension factor is not ad-

Figure 3.2

RATING OF ADVANTAGES OF EMPLOYEE LEASING
(CLIENT INTERVIEWS)

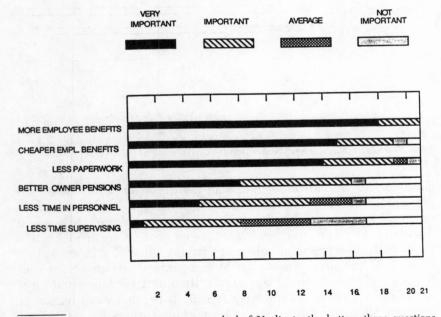

Note: The top three questions were asked of 21 clients; the bottom three questions were asked of 14 clients. Responses that were either not applicable or did not answer the question are not included in this figure.

Source: Office of Advocacy, U.S. Small Business Administration. *Employee Leasing in Small Versus Large Businesses* (Washington, D.C.: SBA, 1986), 47.

dressed, although it obviously plays a part in the thinking of leased employees who currently have such coverage. It is questionable whether small employers will begin asking leasing companies to establish pension plans for their workers now that tax advantaging is not allowed. In fact, leasing company owners indicate that their small clients are *not* asking for pension coverage, primarily because of the cost factor.

Improved Employee Benefits—Costs and Coverage

As illustrated in the case histories, staff leasing firms have the time, expertise, and buying power to purchase employee benefits at lower cost than small employers. Experts such as Browning Group broker Gentry and CEBCOR vice president Crossland indicate that employers generally do not have the group insurance buying power equivalent to that of employee leasing companies unless they have 200 or more employees. Table 3.3 is a worksheet prepared by one staff leasing firm to depict the cost and coverage improvements realized by an actual client. Examination of the medical insurance component alone reveals a savings attributable to the leasing decision that equates to $45 per month per full-time employee.

Table 3.4 illustrates how the 252 employees of the leasing company clients surveyed by Young and Elliott fared with respect to medical and dental coverage before and after leasing. Virtually all those who did not have medical coverage before leasing (about 100 employees) received it as leased workers, and the dental coverage results were even more positive. Young and Elliott also found that

> the medical coverage provided by leasing companies is very comprehensive coverage . . . and is likely to be much better than what the small business owner could obtain on his own. Thus, the medical coverage provided to the 150 employees who had medical coverage before leasing is likely to be better after leasing.[24]

This finding is borne out in Figure 3.3, which shows client perceptions of improvements in various benefits after staff leasing was implemented. As shown in Table 3.5, 132 individuals who did not have group life insurance gained that benefit by becoming leased employees. In addition, individual employees and special groups sometimes benefit, as such, from being leased workers.

Table 3.3

COMPENSATION AND BENEFIT ANALYSIS
FOR A LEASING COMPANY CLIENT

Number of employees: 9   Full Time   1   Part Time

	WEEKLY COSTS	
	Present	Employee Leasing
EMPLOYEE COMPENSATION		
Salary: _____	$3,500.00	$3,500.00
Bonus: _____		
X-Mas Bonus: _____		
Other: _____		
Total: _____	$3,500.00	$3,500.00
BENEFITS		
Uniform Allowance: _____		
Uniforms: _____		
Other: _____		
Insurance		
Medical: *Includes LTD Premium _____	276.92	183.01
Dental: _____		
Disability: _____		24.96
Life: _____		9.76
Malpractice: _____		
Other: _____		
Discount Purchase Program: _____		4.32
Reimbursement Plan: _____		21.15
Dues: _____		
Educational Benefits: _____		
Other: _____		
Total: _____	$ 276.92	$ 243.20
RETIREMENT-Money Purchase Pension Plan 0%	$ 0	$ 0
Pension Plan: _____		
Profit Sharing Plan: _____		
PAYROLL TAXES _____	$ 492.10	$ 436.10
ADMINISTRATIVE COSTS _____	$ 175.00	$ 125.10
TOTALS: _____	$4,444.02	$4,304.40
	126.97%	122.98%

Source: Reprinted with permission of National Employer, Inc.

Table 3.4

NUMBER OF LEASED EMPLOYEES WITH MEDICAL AND DENTAL COVERAGE BEFORE AND AFTER LEASING

Did leased employees have medical coverage before and after leasing?

	Number of Businesses	*Number of Leased Employees*
Before and After	11	151
Not Before but After	10	101
Totals	21	252

Did leased employees have dental coverage before and after leasing?

	Number of Businesses	*Number of Leased Employees*
Before and After	0	0
Not Before but After	21	252
Totals	21	252

Source: Office of Advocacy, U.S. Small Business Administration. *Employee Leasing in Small Versus Large Businesses* (Washington, D.C.: SBA, 1986), 57.

Cited earlier was the situation of two employees who were relieved of high monthly charges for prescription drugs after they became covered by an employee leasing company's insurance plan. Staff Services, Inc., has a small accounting firm client who had been unable to obtain insurance coverage for an employee whose child had diabetes. Under the staff leasing arrangement, the employee now has coverage. Maternity coverage is another area in which benefits are often improved. According to the Browning Group's Gentry, small groups can obtain maternity coverage only with large deductibles, and groups with fewer than three employees cannot obtain it at all.[25] Since women tend to make up a high proportion

Figure 3.3

BENEFITS (CLIENT INTERVIEWS)

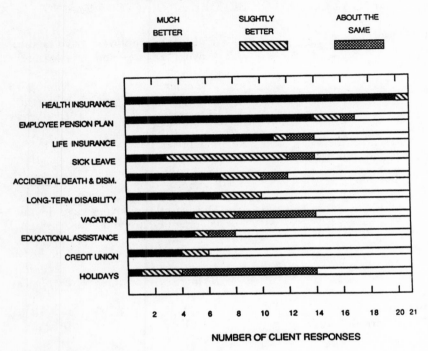

    Notes: No one said that benefits were worse than before they began to use leasing. The top two questions were asked of 21 clients; the bottom eight were asked of 14 clients. Responses that were either not applicable or did not answer the question are not included in this figure.
    Source: Office of Advocacy, U.S. Small Business Administration. *Employee Leasing in Small Versus Large Businesses* (Washington, D.C.: SBA, 1986), p. 55.

of leased employees, leasing is an obvious advantage to them in this respect.

Employee Attitudes

Employees are often apprehensive about terminating their status with a familiar employer and signing on with an "outside" company. But a spokesman for the White Foundation commented with respect to the employees at that organization, "Once they understand the system, they have no complaints."[26] This pattern

Table 3.5

NUMBER OF LEASED EMPLOYEES WITH LIFE INSURANCE BEFORE AND AFTER LEASING

	Did leased employees have life insurance before and after leasing?	
	Number of Businesses	*Number of Leased Employees*
Before and After	3	32
Not Before but After	11	132
Totals	14	164

Source: Office of Advocacy, U.S. Small Business Administration. *Employee Leasing in Small Versus Large Businesses* (Washington, D.C.: SBA, 1986), 58.

is borne out by the research of Young and Elliott. Figures 3.4 and 3.5 illustrate the shift from largely negative to largely positive attitudes as employees become accustomed to the leasing arrangement. The Department of Health and Human Services report labeled as a "misconception" the notion that employees will not accept being leased out, suggesting that "In most cases, acceptance comes after a few paychecks and the issue is forgotten."[27] These positive attitudes seem quite strong. Although accounts other than the work of Young and Elliott are largely anecdotal, they are not difficult to believe. With the high cost of hospital and medical care today, most individuals consider insurance coverage a necessity. To a lesser extent this is also true with regard to disability insurance, pensions, and life insurance.

The translation of these positive attitudes into increased productivity is not, of course, automatic. Traditional motivation theories such as those of Abraham Maslow and Frederick Herzberg[28] classify such benefits as "maintenance factors," or satisfiers of the primary need for security. The presence of basic employee benefits does not motivate employees to apply themselves conscientiously to corporate objectives, but the absence of basic benefits causes problems such as turnover and low productivity and an inclination toward union organizing. In any event, the theories hold, it is difficult, if not impossible, for management to address true, psychic motivation until basic security needs are satisfied. In that sense,

Figure 3.4

EMPLOYEES' INITIAL REACTION TO LEASING
(CLIENT INTERVIEWS)

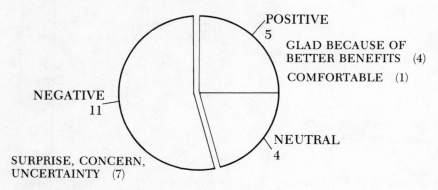

POSITIVE
5

GLAD BECAUSE OF
BETTER BENEFITS   (4)

COMFORTABLE   (1)

NEGATIVE
11

NEUTRAL
4

SURPRISE, CONCERN,
UNCERTAINTY   (7)

FEAR, MISTRUST   (3)

VERY UPSET   (1)

Source: Office of Advocacy, U.S. Small Business Administration.*Employee Leasing in Small Versus Large Businesses* (Washington, D.C.: SBA, 1986), 52.

Figure 3.5

EMPLOYEES' CURRENT REACTION TO LEASING
(CLIENT INTERVIEWS)

POSITIVE
18

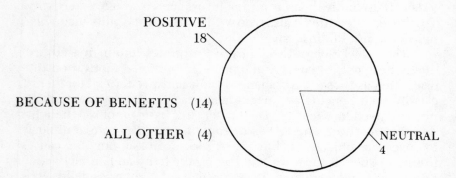

BECAUSE OF BENEFITS   (14)

ALL OTHER   (4)

NEUTRAL
4

Source: Office of Advocacy, U.S. Small Business Administration. *Employee Leasing in Small Versus Large Businesses* (Washington, D.C.: SBA, 1986), 53.

then, the superior benefits accorded workers after their transfer to a leasing firm payroll provide the employer a much improved climate for working toward true motivation.

Another *potential* advantage of staff leasing in terms of employee attitudes is the concept of "portability." Leased employees who do not work out for a given client, or whose jobs with that client are eliminated due to a downturn in business, may be able to be transferred to another client. If they are enrolled in the leasing company's pension plan, they do not lose credited service in that case because they remain employees of the leasing firm and members of the plan. At a minimum, the leasing company may offer outplacement assistance as part of its contract with the client. While professional and managerial employees have traditionally had employment agencies, search firms, and their professional and alumni associations to fall back on, blue-collar workers rarely have such resources. The leasing arrangement thus provides them at least some new measure of job security. However, although leasing companies can cite success stories, most of them do not yet have sufficiently large employee pools or demand to make portability a common occurrence.

Personnel Services

The "personnel packages" offered by full-service employee leasing firms are perceived to be highly advantageous by clients. In addition to the recruiting and employee benefits functions already cited, the benefits of leasing company personnel services can be thought of in terms of three general components: structure, consultation, and intervention.

To give structure to the employment relationship, most employee leasing firms provide employee handbooks spelling out personnel and employee benefits policies and procedures. They also have formal grievance procedures and performance appraisal systems, and they may develop job descriptions with their clients as an aid to recruitment, performance evaluation, and job evaluation. (The performance appraisals are conducted by leasing company field supervisors based on input provided by the client. The field supervisors play both a consultative and administrative role here, notifying the client as appraisals are due, providing forms, and giving guidance as necessary.) Many small businesses have none, or only a few, of these human resource management tools. In the public sector, the Department of Health and Human Services has noted that "if the leasing concept were to be used to consolidate, streamline or specialize CSE [Child Support Enforcement] functions, then the workers [would] have better defined tasks and work standards with which to fulfill their assigned missions."[29]

Leasing firms may play a valuable mediator role by intervening in work-related conflicts between clients and employees. As CEBCOR's Crossland points out, many small business owners are "the iron-fisted type" who may act precipitously when an employee incurs their displeasure. A CEBCOR spokesman indicated that on a "fairly routine basis," its field supervisors counsel both parties independently when there is conflict, and they work out courses of action to "modify behavior by both parties." Marvin Selter, of National Staff Leasing, refers to the leasing firm as a "safety valve" in this respect, relieving the client of time-consuming, stress-producing, and legally precarious actions that can accompany termination of employment.

Minimizing legal exposure is increasingly important in view of the continuing judicial erosion of the traditional employment-at-will doctrine. State courts have rendered large damage awards against employers in "unjust dismissal" suits brought by fired employees.[30] According to the San Francisco law firm of Schachter, Kristoff, Ross, Sprague & Curiale, plaintiffs received favorable verdicts in 78 percent of wrongful discharge jury trials in California in 1986. The average total award was $424,527.[31] Staff leasing firms, like other large companies, have the resources to track the developing case law in this new expansion of employee rights, and they know the steps to take to minimize vulnerability to claims of wrongful dismissal. Most small business owners probably are not even aware that such a danger exists; yet, they have the most to lose. Six-figure damage awards, or even legal fees in such cases, could be devastating to small and medium-size businesses. It should be noted that even such basic tools as written job descriptions, job evaluation plans, grievance procedures, and other uniform personnel policies can minimize a company's exposure to work-related legal problems. Full-service staff leasing firms have these tools in place.

Quality and Continuity of Staffing

Quality and continuity of staffing have three closely related components that are favorably affected by employee leasing: personnel turnover rates, timely filling of job vacancies, and quality of personnel hired.

There are no formal studies comparing turnover rates between comparable groups of leased workers and those employed directly by the company for whom they work. The BNA special report did include a comment by a principal of the White Memorial Otolaryngology Foundation, Los Angeles, to which a large staff leasing firm supplies approximately 100 employees at four locations. The leasing agreement has been in effect since 1972. The principal, a practicing physician, remarked that over the 10 years he had been associated with the foundation, 30 to 40 percent of the original personnel had remained. He noted that those figures represent a low turnover rate for a doctor's office.[32] (A 6- to 7-percent annual turnover rate is good in nearly *any* type of business or professional organization.) While the doctor's observation does not prove cause and effect, it seems safe to assume that the benefits enjoyed by employees of relatively large leasing firms contribute to lessened job hopping. This may be especially true at lower skill levels, where even a small increase in wages may justify changing jobs in the absence of meaningful employee benefits.

The employee leasing client can expect prompt service in filling job vacancies created by turnover. It is not the client's employee who has left, but that of the leasing firm. It is therefore the latter's responsibility to secure a replacement promptly. With respect to additional staff needs, the leasing company may either draw on its existing pool of employees or begin recruiting. Because it routinely recruits on behalf of clients—writing and placing recruitment advertisements and screening résumés—it is likely to come up with suitable candidates more quickly than could the small business owners it serves.

Finally, if having comprehensive employee benefits and services helps small business owners hold their own in competing against larger companies for skilled personnel, it also gives them a decided advantage over their small business competitors. The owner of an air-conditioning business, an industry in which there is great competition for skilled employees, was quoted by Naisbitt and Aburdene as saying, "A lot of my competition doesn't have health and pension plans, so my company attracts the best people. Now the only people who leave here are those who are asked to leave."[33]

Wage Costs and Administration

Replacing an employer-employee relationship with a staff leasing agreement does not affect wage and salary rates per se. In contrast to temporary employees, the workers remain as regular, permanent employees, so their rates of pay are influenced by the same general factors as applied before the leasing arrangement. However, a full-service staff leasing firm may increase the effectiveness of the former employer's compensation dollar indirectly. Many small business owners do not have up-to-date information about prevailing wage rates or comparability of jobs. If employees leave "for more money," or a "better job," the owner can only guess what that means. If other employees are overpaid, of course, they are not likely to volunteer that information. Since employee leasing companies, like THS firms, are in the personnel business, they may recruit and compete in many labor markets; therefore they must remain abreast of compensation rates and trends. They recommend to their clients adjustments both in rates for various job categories and in compensation plan design. Some conduct area or industry salary surveys for specific clients.

There is an element of objectivity here, as well. Many small business owners have closer employer-employee relationships than occur in the management of large corporations. They often employ relatives, and they find it difficult to deny wage increases to employees who have been at their side through good times and bad or to individuals who request salary increases based on personal hardship. The leasing firm can play the role often assumed by consultants in these instances, bringing compensation practices into line with marketplace realities, and supporting its recommendation with objective data.

Services performed by the leasing company may affect total payroll in other ways. Bartex, Inc., the Dallas construction firm cited earlier, has eliminated one job from its accounting department after turning over to CEBCOR responsibility for payroll and personnel paperwork.[34]

Overall Cost Reduction

Table 3.6 is a leasing company's depiction of how one of its clients saved an amount equal to about 5 percent of gross payroll through staff leasing. The savings were in the areas of direct personnel administration costs and employee benefit costs. The Department of Health and Human Services estimates that "an average manager may spend from 7 to 23 percent of his/her time handling the required non-productive employee-related administrative paperwork."[35] These figures will, of course, vary with individual circumstances; in some instances, leasing may prove more expensive.

Table 3.6

COMPARISON OF COSTS FOR TYPICAL
SEVEN-EMPLOYEE GROUP

Current Owner/Professional Costs		*National Employer Costs*
Gross Monthly Payroll	100.0%	100.0%
Payroll Taxes	13.8%	13.8%
Administrative Costs	7.0%	4.5%
Pension Costs	0.0%	3.0%
Other Benefits Costs	13.4%	9.4%
Intangible Costs (Aggravation, Away From Business, etc.)	?	-0-
Total	134.2%	130.7%

SAVE UP TO 5% ON EMPLOYEE COSTS

Source: National Employer, Inc.

As suggested by the question mark following the item "Intangible Costs," the figures do not reflect the indirect savings of freeing the business owner from personnel matters. These indirect savings should be given special attention by the small business owner. For the corporate line manager, a certain amount of personnel work is part of the job; the small entrepreneur, however, is adversely affected by every hour spent on staff work. Small businesses are particularly vulnerable to business losses. It is essential, then, that working owners devote as much time as possible to the core functions of marketing, product or service development, customer contact, production, and use of their professional skills.

Disadvantages of Staff Leasing

Legal Issues

Liabilities Under Labor Law

Business owners who effectively maintain control of personnel decisions after the work force is leased may find themselves in serious trouble if the leasing company fails to make payroll or fails to withhold and remit taxes and other legally required payments. The same holds true with respect to legal actions brought by or on behalf of employees under statutes such as the National Labor Relations Act (NLRA) and various nondiscrimination laws. Attorney R.J. James, of Squire, Sanders and Dempsey, notes that, traditionally, and under the NLRA and Fair Labor Standards Act (FLSA) in particular, the term *independent contractor* has been construed very narrowly because its invocation has been seen as a device by which employers sought to avoid paying overtime or to prevent employees from organizing.

> Under the NLRA, it doesn't matter what you call people— you can call them leased employees or anything you like—it's what they are. And if they are in fact your employees, they have a right to protest, and picketing is, under certain circumstances, legal and appropriate.
>
> Where an employer terminates his employees and leases them back from a leasing company, they could still be held to be employees of that employer for purposes of organizing rights under the NLRA.

James also points out the possible implications in such areas as workers' compensation:

> If workers on a company's premises are truly the employees of an independent contractor, workers' compensation claims should not be a major concern to the contractor's client; the responsibility for workers' compensation rests with the contractor. However, if it is found that an injured worker involved in such an arrangement is an employee of that employer, for purposes of workers' compensation, the employer may fare far worse than he or she would have if prepared with workers' compensation and/or liability insurance. In addition to providing adequate insurance coverage, prudent employers can, through their carriers and service firms, investigate and somewhat control workers' compensation claims filed by their employees. The employer who contracts for workers misses this opportunity for front-end control and fact finding; it "isn't his problem."
>
> If the agency supplying the worker lacks expertise in this area, and the employer winds up with legal responsibility for a claim, he or she may have to pay for a claim and/or judgment that would have been disallowed if [the employer] had been in control at the onset.

Indemnification

Some leasing companies insist on "hold harmless" or "indemnification" clauses in their client contracts. For example, the standard contract of one leasing firm first establishes that it is an independent contractor and that it is the employer of all employees assigned to the client. The contract further provides that the leasing company has "the sole responsibility for recruiting, hiring, evaluating, replacing, supervising, disciplining and firing of individuals assigned to Client's Job Function Positions." This is fairly standard language in staff leasing contracts. However, later in the agreement there is an indemnification clause that reads as follows:

> Client hereby agrees to indemnify and hold harmless [leasing company] against any and all damages, liability, cost or expenses, including attorneys' fees which arise out of or from any injury or damage to person or property as a result of any action or failure to take action by the Client, its servants, agents, employees, guests, licensees and contractors, *including the aforementioned assigned employees*, except as covered by workers' compensation insurance. . . . (Emphasis supplied.)[36]

These two clauses seem to put the client in the precarious position of surrendering control of its employees to the leasing firm while accepting accountability for the results. Because such an arrangement violates a fundamental management principle—matching of accountability with authority—it could prove extremely expensive to the leasing company client.

The situation can become even more tenuous when the business owner is also an employee of the leasing company. If, as in many leasing agreements, the leasing firm is obliged to consult with "the client" in the selection of employees and "the client" may have the leasing company remove an employee it deems unsatisfactory, with whom, acting on behalf of the client corporation, does the leasing firm consult in these matters? That this question appears unanswerable illustrates the point: The business owner who is an employee of a major supplier has an untenable conflict of interest that could have untold legal consequences. Some leasing firms refuse to employ their clients because they see the conflict of interest as potentially harmful to themselves as well. For example, some indemnification clauses state that the client will indemnify and hold the leasing firm harmless from damages arising from "the client's" violation of health and safety and other state and federal labor laws. If all the persons who direct the client's operations are employed and supervised by the leasing company, who is there to commit such violations as an agent of the client?

The Control Issue

Employers in the most precarious position, then, are the ones who have been deluded into thinking that, through the leasing arrangement, they can have their cake and eat it too. But employers who recognize this danger and seek to establish either a conservative arrangement of the kind advocated by National Staff Leasing's Marvin Selter or a defined joint employer contract, must decide how much control they can give up and what the implications may be for their firms. (They also miss out on the improved employee benefits enjoyed by the leased workers.) Suppose, for example, a leased employee commits a safety infraction that the client considers a dischargeable offense, but the leasing company does not. How many entrepreneurs will accept the leasing firm's dictate that "he stays"? Selter advised BNA that when a client wants an employee removed without adequate cause, "we'll get rid of the client."[37] When the leasing firm has complete control over staffing, it could reassign the client's former employees to work for other clients, replacing them with workers who are qualified in the leasing company's judgment—not the client's.

Questionable Operators in the Staff Leasing Industry

Speaking to the National Staff Leasing Association in 1985, James Swartzwelder, then acting director of the IRS Planning Office, stated,

> Leasing companies are going into business with relatively few assets and very quickly accumulating large pension benefit, employment and withheld income tax liabilities, and then failing and leaving those liabilities unpaid. It's very, very important to look carefully at who you're dealing with.[38]

Young and Elliott explained that leasing companies make some of their money from the float between the time when they collect funds from their clients and when they pay them out. "Some leasing companies, however, succumb to the temptation of using some of these funds to finance normal office operations. . . . It is very difficult to repay these funds given the industry's traditionally low profit margin."[39] As Keith Crossland of CEBCOR put it, some employee leasing firms are "a couple of guys and an office."

Lending credence to the fact that employers should proceed with caution in selecting staff leasing companies, Young and Elliott encountered the following in the course of their research:

- When they sought to contact 49 leasing companies listed in *The Directory of Employee Leasing Companies* for the San

Francisco Bay Area and greater Los Angeles, they could not find a phone number for 12 of them. [40]
- When they asked leasing companies about their average monthly premiums for single and family medical coverage, 10 of 19 companies queried did not know, and 6 would not answer. [41]
- Of the 14 firms in the sample, 2 were not sure whether they had fiduciary responsibility insurance in case of errors made in administering employee benefit programs. [42]

While industry leaders such as Selter would like to see a shakeout of what he calls "blue suede shoe operators," there are as yet no requirements for entry into the staff leasing business.

Limited Availability of Compatible Leasing Firms

Because of the geographic concentration of staff leasing firms, a company may not have the option of engaging one. If leasing firms *are* in the employer's area, they may not choose to do business with it. Young and Elliott found that in addition to preferring not to serve high-turnover industries, some leasing companies avoid seasonal firms, high-accident industries such as construction, and union-related industries. [43]

The Leasing Decision and Its Implementation

Assuming that leasing companies are available, a company interested in exploring staff leasing might proceed along the lines suggested in the following paragraphs. These recommendations are not intended to be all-inclusive, nor should they necessarily be addressed in the order given; they are better thought of as a partial checklist than a procedure.

Set Goals

As with other alternative employment strategies, staff leasing should be approached as a means toward accomplishing specific goals. In formulating those goals, management might use the tables in this chapter as a model for ranking the potential advantages of leasing in the form of goal statements, for example, eliminate the payroll function; reduce the percentage of owner's time spent in doing personnel paperwork; and provide better benefits. Current costs of performing those functions and tasks in house can then be calculated. For example, if 50 percent of a clerical person's time is spent on payroll and 5 percent of the owner's time on personnel matters, costs can be assigned. Management may wish to value those hours in terms of opportunity costs. One might reason, for example; "If I could devote the 300 hours a year I spend on personnel work to calling on new customers, I could create $75,000 in new business." For less tangible factors such as the effect of improved employee benefits, the manager or owner may wish to make an assumption about the potential savings associated with, say, a 25-percent reduction in employee turnover. Even if recruitment costs will be borne by the leasing firm, replacing turnovers with new employees means orientation and training time and more errors.

Seek Legal Counsel

It has been shown that employee leasing can be a legal mine field. Counsel should advise management on the crucial issue of how much management control it must give up to attain a certain degree of safety from liability, and management must then decide how much it *wants* to give up. Consultant Arno and others in the industry emphasize that staff leasing is not for everyone. For both psychological and operating reasons, management may be unwilling or unable to surrender real control over its work force. The key is to come to this realization *before* entering into a leasing agreement—not after. Young and Elliott found that six out of seven of the leasing firms they interviewed had cancelled client contracts because the clients did not follow their rules, were difficult to work with, or did not pay for services.[44]

The freedom implied in the employer's option to cancel the staff leasing contract upon 30 days' notice may be illusory. It is difficult to imagine a more chaotic situation. When the client signs on with the leasing company, it terminates its employees and its benefits converge; it dismantles the payroll system and all related record-keeping systems. Having a leasing firm drop out of the picture in that situation could put a small employer out of business.

Secure Proposals

Establish Leasing Company Qualifications

Where feasible, management should discuss its needs with several competing staff leasing firms and solicit competitive proposals. A leasing firm is not just another vendor. There is a potential for significant employee relations problems and financial liabilities for the client in the event of the leasing firm's failure to live up to its obligations. Accordingly, each proposal should contain detailed background information about the leasing firm, its principals, and their experience. References should be provided. Management should talk personally with other clients of the leasing firms and should ask the leasing firms for the names of clients who may have discontinued their services, as well. Credit information should be obtained and, if possible, an audited statement of financial condition.

Determine Charges and Services

The proposal should detail the specific services to be provided and relevant time frames—for example, the time period within which replacement employees will be made available. All deposits, fees, charges, and fund transfers should be spelled out in detail. Start-up costs and time commitments should be detailed. For example, how much time will the account representative spend on site to become familiar with operations, present the leasing program to the employees, answer questions, and so forth? Will there be a special charge for this? Will written job descriptions be necessary? If so, will the leasing company charge for its time spent in the effort? The leasing company's complete employee benefits package should be part of the proposal. It should include pay for time-not-worked benefits such as vacations, holidays, and paid sick leave.

Define Supervision

In evaluating proposals, management may want to look closely at the number of field supervisors available relative to the number of leased workers on the company's payroll. Young and Elliott found, for example, that the supervisor-to-employee ratio varied from 1:50 to 1:150; frequency of contact varied from once a quarter to twice a month.[45] The minimum frequency with which the leasing firm's field supervisor will visit the client site should be specified. If employees have questions between supervisors' visits or wish to file grievances, whom do they call . . . at whose expense?

Identify Account Representative

The working relationship between the client owner-manager and the leasing company account representative (who sometimes acts as the field supervisor as well) is a sensitive one because of the inherent "turf" issue. The client should know who that individual will be and develop a rapport before an agreement is signed. Although it may balk at putting it in writing, the leasing firm will probably agree informally not to assign the client a different account manager without the latter's approval (unless, of course, the original account manager leaves the firm).

Spell Out Insurance Coverage

Leasing companies may provide several kinds of insurance coverage, including employee bonding, workers' compensation, general liability, professional liability, and fiduciary responsibility. Legal relationships and responsibilities can become complex in this area, and the client should involve its insurance carriers in reviewing these aspects of the proposal.

Obtain Independent Verification of Performance

The client should insist that the staff leasing firm furnish at least quarterly verification from a CPA or PA firm that the leasing company has made all withholdings and payments required by law and all employee benefit contributions required by the leasing agreement and/or ERISA. Leasing companies that are members of the National Staff Leasing Association and the National Staff Network are required to do this under the bylaws of those organizations. Exhibit 3.1 is a sample verification letter recommended by that organization.

Exhibit 3.1

INDEPENDENT AUDITOR'S OPINION LETTER IN FORMAT SUGGESTED BY NATIONAL STAFF LEASING ASSOCIATION

HaUSSER✛TaYLOR

CERTIFIED PUBLIC ACCOUNTANTS, 1000 EATON CENTER, CLEVELAND, OHIO 44114, (216) 523-1900

To The Stockholders
National Employer, Inc.
Cleveland, Ohio

At your request, we have performed the procedures enumerated below with respect to the payroll of National Employer, Inc. as of March 31, 1986. Our report was made for the sole purpose of examining the procedures followed by National Employer, Inc. relating to the payroll and related benefits of its employees. The procedures performed related to determining the following:

a. We determined that Federal, State and Local payroll taxes have been deposited on a timely basis as required by the appropriate government authority.

b. We determined that health and other related employee benefits provided by the company have been paid on a current and timely basis.

c. We determined that pension plan contributions are being made as provided under the plans.

In connection with the procedures referred to above, no matters came to our attention that caused us to believe that the specified items should be adjusted. This report relates only to the items specified above and does not extend to any financial statements of National Employer, Inc.

Hausser + Taylor

Cleveland, Ohio
May 27, 1986

Members of the American Institute of Certified Public Accountants

| CLEVELAND | CANTON | COLUMBUS | ELYRIA | MEDINA |

Source: Reprinted with permission of National Employer, Inc.

Communicate With Employees

No matter how it is expressed, the message to employees that they are to be terminated will be unsettling. To the extent that management can anticipate concerns and address them effectively, they will be minimized. The leasing firm should make recommendations for employee communications as part of its proposal. Since the primary task will fall to the employer, however, the communications effort should reflect the employer's style, whatever the supporting role played by the leasing company. One method for overcoming employees' initial mistrust or misgivings is to arrange for them to get together with other employees of the leasing company—ideally, people from the same community who have made the transition successfully.

Explore Alternatives to Staff Leasing

With detailed proposals in hand, the employer can begin to estimate the net effect of various employee leasing arrangements in terms of its qualitative and quantitative goals. The employer can also use this information to evaluate the costs of alternatives to staff leasing. Adoption of personal-computer-based human resource information systems, use of employment agencies, and group insurance programs offered through local employer associations are options that might accomplish some of the desired goals. Any agreement reached with a leasing company should be thoroughly reviewed by counsel as it takes shape and before it is executed.

The Future of Employee Leasing

Possible Legislation

Most experts agree that staff leasing's break with tax advantaging will benefit the industry by removing what Young and Elliott call the "stigma of possible 'tax scam.' "[46] However, divorcing staff leasing from safe-harbor pension plans does not necessarily mean that the industry will face no further attempts by federal and state legislators to regulate it. As suggested by Swartzwelder, of the IRS, and others, there is a potential for staff leasing companies to misuse large sums of withheld taxes.

Because of that concern, the IRS is studying the records of all known staff leasing firms in the Laguna Niguel, California, Dallas, and Hartford districts regarding deposits of taxes withheld from leased employees. Data from the study were to be sent to the national office of the IRS by April 1, 1987.[47]

In January 1987, independent of the IRS study, U.S. Congressman Schultze of Pennsylvania introduced House Bill (H.R.) 246, which has been referred to the Committee on Ways and Means. Among other things, the bill would amend the Internal Revenue Code of 1986 to mandate standards for employee leasing companies seeking to offer safe-harbor pension plans. The regulations would require leasing firms to adopt key elements of the "conservative" approach described earlier in this chapter. Under Section 8 of the bill, the leasing organization must meet the following requirements, among others, to qualify as the "sole employer" of a leased employee:

- retain the sole and exclusive right to hire, terminate, and transfer the employee;
- pay the employee from its own account; and
- direct, control, and evaluate the manner and means of the employee's performance of services to the recipient (client).

In addition, the bill would require the leasing organization to be responsible for paying its employees regardless of receiving fees from the client and to bill the client on a total-fee rather than a direct-cost-passthrough basis. Section 9 of the bill would require the Secretary of the Treasury to prescribe regulations to ensure prompt reporting and depositing of withholding and employment taxes by the leasing organization and to maximize timely IRS monitoring of such reporting and depositing. Such regulations would include identifying each leasing firm by Standard Industry Code (SIC) and requiring firms to register with the IRS, including registration of all officers, equity owners, and other principals.

If the IRS study reveals substantial misuse of funds by the leasing firms under scrutiny, reform along the lines of H.R. 246 will be all the more likely. A number of other regulations might emerge from such legislation; for example, leasing companies might be required to deposit payroll tax and pension funds into trust accounts. As pointed out by Young and Elliott, such a requirement will not insure against bankruptcy or mishandling of monies, but "will go a long way toward removing temptation from leasing firm operators and towards insuring that these funds are still available should a firm go bankrupt."[48] Given the seriousness of the issues involved—in terms of both financial liabilities and employee relations—it is difficult to imagine that such requirements would do anything but benefit clients of staff leasing firms. The requirements might also hasten the "shakeout" of questionable operators sought by Selter and other leaders in the industry.

Factors Suggesting Continued Growth

Assuming that the staff leasing industry is not encumbered by *overly* restrictive regulation, it will in all likelihood continue to grow in popularity as an alternative to the conventional employment relationship. Increasing numbers of businesses are no longer viewing employment as a "relationship," but as an unwelcome and unproductive entanglement. As personnel administration of regular staff becomes riskier, costlier, and more complicated due to legislation such as COBRA, the 1987 Immigration Act, and, perhaps, family leave requirements, there will be more incentive for small employers to contract personnel chores to staff leasing companies. The increased national emphasis on competitiveness, including large-company pressures on small suppliers for "just-in-time inventory," lower prices, and higher quality, will force small business owners to focus on operations rather than paperwork and personnel problems.

Larger and medium-size firms may also benefit from staff leasing. Consultant Arno notes that some hotel chains are considering drawing on a staff leasing company's pool of maids, waiters, and other service people as their individual volume warrants it. One staff leasing firm is negotiating with a construction employers' association in Southern California to establish a similar labor pool.

There is a need for improved management productivity in the public sector, as well. The Department of Health and Human Services has concluded that *"It is increasingly important for a decision maker to concentrate on production-oriented activities,"*[49] noting the potential of staff leasing arrangements to free managers' time for such activities.

Notes

1. L.A. Young and E.S. Elliott, *Employee Leasing in Small Versus Large Businesses.* Report prepared for the Office of Advocacy, U.S. Small Business Administration (Washington, D.C.: SBA, 1986), 9.
2. S.S. Cohen, "Employee Leasing: Industry in a Time of Change," *The Forum*, 20 (4), Summer 1985, 661.

3. H. Bacas, "Leasing People," *Nation's Business*, October 1984, 57.
4. J. Fierman, "Employees Learn to Love Being Leased Out," *Fortune*, 1 April 1985, 80.
5. J. Naisbitt and P. Aburdene, *Re-inventing the Corporation* (New York: Warner Books, 1985), 61.
6. T. J. Murray, "Employee Leasing: Fast Growth—And Trouble," *Dun's Business Month*, July 1984, 69.
7. M. Fletcher, "Leasing Employees Raises Liability Worries," *Business Insurance*, 2 December 1985, 20.
8. P. Sellers, "Omnistaff's Lease Runs Out," *Fortune*, 9 December 1985, 11.
9. Until early 1987, the firm was known as "Office Staff Services, Inc." It is referred to frequently as "Office Staff Services, Inc.," in the Health and Human Services report cited in note 13.
10. A. Bennett, "Tax Legislation Puts Leasing of Employees in a New Light," *The Wall Street Journal*, 9 September 1986, 27.
11. Bureau of National Affairs, Inc., *Flexible Staffing*. Exclusive Results of a Survey on U.S. Firms' Use of Non-Regular Employees. Special supplement to BNA's *Employee Relations Weekly*, 8 September 1986.
12. The BNA special supplement cited in note 11 reported preliminarily that Young and Elliott surveyed 37 leasing company clients (p. 32); as published, the Young and Elliott report was based on a survey of 21 leasing company clients (p. 1).
13. Department of Health and Human Services, Family Support Administration, Office of Child Support Enforcement, "Use of Employee Contract Services as a Management Tool for Resource Expansion and Inter-Jurisdictional Operational Enhancements" (Washington, D.C.: 1986). Released as an attachment to Information Memorandum OCSE-IM-86-06 of 18 September 1986.
14. Young and Elliott, *Employee Leasing*, note 1, above, 15.
15. Ibid., 32.
16. Ibid., 39.
17. Ibid., 50.
18. Ibid., 31.
19. From text of a prepared statement given before the Subcommittee on Select Revenue Measures, Committee on Ways and Means, U.S. House of Representatives, Washington, D.C., 12 May 1986, 1 (emphasis supplied by Mr. Selter).
20. Department of Health and Human Services, "Use of Employee Contract Services," note 13, above. (Emphasis from the original; note also the agency's use of quotation marks around the word *transfers*.)
21. Bureau of National Affairs, Inc., *The Changing Workplace: New Directions in Staffing and Scheduling*. Special Report (Washington, D.C.: BNA, 1986), 33.
22. Young and Elliott, *Employee Leasing*, note 1, above, 46.
23. Ibid., 47.
24. Ibid., 54.
25. A. Bennett, "Tax Legislation," note 10, above, 27.
26. BNA, *The Changing Workplace*, note 21, above, 35.
27. Department of Health and Human Services, "Use of Employee Contract Services," note 13, above, 2.
28. See for example, F. Herzberg, "One More Time: How Do You Motivate Employees?" *Harvard Business Review*, January–February 1968, 53–62; and

A.H. Maslow, "A Theory of Human Motivation," *Psychological Review*, Vol. 50, 1943, 370–396.

29. Department of Health and Human Services, "Use of Employee Contract Services," note 13, above, 6.
30. See D. Nye, "Fire At Will—Careful Now, Careful," *Across the Board*, November 1982.
31. C. Trost, Labor Letter Column, *The Wall Street Journal*, March 3, 1987, 1.
32. BNA, *The Changing Workplace*, note 21, above, 35, 36.
33. Naisbitt and Aburdene, *Re-inventing*, note 5, above, 62.
34. A. Bennett, "Tax Legislation," note 10, above, 27.
35. Department of Health and Human Services, "Use of Employee Contract Services," note 13, above, 1.
36. Ibid., unmarked exhibit. The document is a sample client contract used by a Florida staff leasing firm.
37. BNA, *The Changing Workplace*, note 21, above, 35.
38. Ibid., 33.
39. Young and Elliott, *Employee Leasing*, note 1, above, 65.
40. Ibid., A-7.
41. Ibid., 29.
42. Ibid., 24.
43. Ibid., 19.
44. Ibid., 32.
45. Ibid., 21.
46. Ibid., 60.
47. "Employee Leasing Draws the Critical Eye of the IRS in a Compliance Study," *The Wall Street Journal*, 18 March 1987, 1.
48. Young and Elliott, *Employee Leasing*, note 1, above, 66.
49. Department of Health and Human Services, "Use of Employee Contract Services," note 13, above, 1. (Emphasis from the original.)

4

Retirees and Older Employees

The Aging U.S. Work Force

Human-resources professionals seeking a grasp of the issues bearing on employment of older workers are not alone in their quest. In recent years, industry and public opinion surveys; academic and congressional studies; and economic, demographic, and psychographic data have been prepared, commissioned, analyzed, and published by experts, advocates, and the popular press seeking to identify the short- and long-term consequences of an aging population. The picture is somewhat confused because there is no standard definition of "older worker." The federal Age Discrimination in Employment Act (ADEA) protects employees age 40 and over; the federal Administration on Aging uses age 55 and above in referring to older workers; and the U.S. Department of Labor designates employees over age 40 as "mature workers." Significant public and business opinion surveys have used age 50 and above in referring to "older Americans." This book will refer to men and women age 50 and above when speaking generally of "older," "mature," or "senior" workers.

Whatever definition is used, there is little question that the aging of the populace has major implications for employers. The following facts and projections suggest just a few dimensions of the phenomenon:

- In 1982, 48 million Americans were age 55 or over; of those, 26 million were 65 or older. In the next 30 years, the number of Americans age 55 and over will climb to 70 million; they will then represent 1 in 4 persons. Fully half of that group will be age 65 and above.

- By the year 2030, nearly 30 percent of the population will be at least age 55; 55 million of them will be age 65 and over, and of those, 40 percent—or 22 million—will be age 75 and over. The 65-and-over group will then compose 18 percent of the population.

- As these changes occur, life expectancies will continue to increase. Current male life expectancy at birth is 70 years, and men who reach age 65 can expect to live to age 74. For men born in 2010, those figures will increase to 73 and 81, respectively. There will be similar increases in women's longevity; by the year 2010, their life expectancy at birth will be nearly 82 years, and those who reach 65 can expect to live almost 22 additional years. Some experts suggest that if current life-style trends continue, that is, increased exercise and decreased smoking, drinking, and cholesterol intake, we will see even higher life expectancies than those now projected.

- Not only are people living longer chronologically, they are living "younger" in terms of relative health and vigor. Alan Pifer, president emeritus of the Carnegie Corporation, put it simply: "People are much younger now, at older ages, than they were previously."[1]

  This phenomenon, verified by the experience of companies that have never had mandatory retirement, led one expert to conclude: "If a chronologically meaningful retirement age were to be selected today, it would have to be made at least a decade later than would have made sense 20 years ago."[2]

- Between 1982 and the year 2000, we will have experienced a reduction of 8.3 million persons in the 18-to-34 age range, a group that represents a substantial portion of the current work force. There will be a concomitant increase of some 27 million in the 35-to-50 age range.[3]

- With a few narrow exceptions, Congress has outlawed mandatory retirement.

- A Harris poll released in 1979 found that 48 percent of workers age 50 to 64 expected to work after 65; 46 percent of retirees polled said they would prefer to be working; and 53 percent of them wished they had not retired.

These data seem to suggest longer work force participation by individuals, but the following cross-currents must also be considered:

- A 1979 study by the President's Council on Pension Policy found that nearly half the working population expected to retire at age 62 or before.[4]
- Despite fluctuations in employment rates and increases in the mandatory retirement age under federal law, participation of older persons in the work force has dropped steadily and dramatically. In 1979, only 62 percent of men age 60 to 64 were in the labor force compared to 75 percent in 1970 and 78 percent in 1960 (see Figure 4.1); the average retirement age is now under 62.
- The radical restructuring of large and medium-size companies continues. That restructuring brings with it the disappearance of millions of relatively well-compensated jobs typically held by workers of "prime" working age (defined by the Department of Labor as 35 to 54). Eleven million jobs were lost in heavy industry alone between 1979 and 1984. Hundreds of thousands of older workers have abruptly left their jobs and careers under "voluntary" early retirement plans that are usually precursors to major reductions in force.
- A Conference Board study published in January 1985 found that the great majority of the 363 companies polled encourage retirement at age 65; 60 percent include early retirement inducements in their pension plans, and only 3 percent offer employees any incentive to remain on the job beyond age 65.[5]

Mixed Conclusions

As suggested by this modest data sample, there is a sea of information available on older workers and related issues, but it is mined with anomaly and paradox. A U.S. Department of Labor expert explains,

There is lively debate concerning the labor force implications of such an "older" population . . . because so many considerations influence the choice which older persons make between work and retirement—such as availability of retirement benefits, health status, job opportunities, training and education, and

Figure 4.1

LABOR FORCE PARTICIPATION RATE
AND UNEMPLOYMENT RATE
Males 55–64
1961–1979

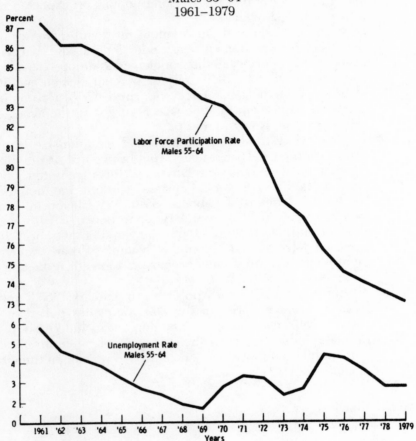

Source: U.S. Congress, Senate Special Committee on Aging, *Work After 65: Options for the 80's: Hearing Before the Special Committee on Aging*, 96th Cong., 2d Sess., 13 May 1980 (Washington: U.S. Government Printing Office),   135. Taken from Dept. of Labor, Bureau of Statistics, *Handbook of Labor Statistics*, 1975 and 1977. Employment and Earnings, January 1979, January 1980.

personal preferences—it is difficult to draw reasonable conclusions about the future age composition of the labor force. This problem becomes more complicated because economic conditions, which directly affect aggregate demand for labor, cannot be predicted with certainty.[6]

Private-sector experts agree, pointing out that the federal government has added much to the confusion. There is no coherent federal policy or legislative agenda on retirement and related issues. In the past few years there have been successive amendments to the Age Discrimination in Employment Act, tinkering with the Social Security system and private pension regulations, and alternating encouragement and restriction of individual retirement account (IRA) and 401(k) plans. These actions have sent mixed and contradictory signals to corporate pension and human resource planners and to older workers themselves.

Employer Views

Many employers have complicated the picture with conflicting policies and practices regarding mature workers. What most often results is that the benefits of progressive, profit-oriented programs are quietly undone by old policies based on negative stereotypes about the abilities, attitudes, and potential of mature workers. For example, thousands of companies have implemented employee "wellness" programs that include physical fitness and life-style evaluations, exercise facilities and instruction, smoking cessation and weight loss clinics, and other health education programs and services. Enthusiastic corporate officials proclaim wellness programs as highly cost-effective, and they do indeed seem to pay off in a healthier, more vigorous, productive, and committed work force. Using a human resources accounting model, it could be said that these companies have made a thoughtful investment in upgrading the long-term capacity of their human assets.

The retirement policies of these same firms, however, have "written off" many of these newly refurbished assets through "accelerated depreciation" in the form of early retirement incentives. Many of the remaining human assets have then been "scrapped," forced to retire at the earliest moment permitted by law. In 1984, for example, employees at Standard Oil Company headquarters in Cleveland, Ohio, were encouraged to sign up for extensive medical, life-style, and physical fitness evaluations. The main purpose of the evaluations was to permit employees to use safely and productively an elaborate physical fitness center being readied in the company's new, $200 million headquarters building. The center was just part of an extensive wellness program already under way. The business purpose of the program was to increase long-term employee productivity and decrease employment costs by helping employees eliminate or reduce well-known risks to health and well-being. At the same time as they were receiving invitations to sign up for the wellness program, however, senior employees were receiving notice of a one-time early retirement plan that offered them special incentives to leave the company.

Not only are there inconsistencies among policies, gaps are sometimes found between policy and practice regarding the older worker. In a survey by Yankelovich, Skelly, and White, Inc., 48 percent of the responding human resource executives and CEOs said that skill training for older workers would be an effective management tool. However, only 30 percent of their companies had begun implementing such programs. While 43 percent recognized continued part-time work for older workers as an effective way to leverage their skills, only 18 percent had such programs in place. (See Figures 4.2 and 4.3.)

Figure 4.2

APPROACHES TO TRAINING AND THE OLDER WORKER

All Companies

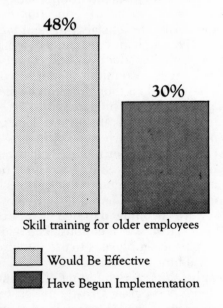

Source: American Association of Retired Persons. Adapted from *Workers Over 50: Old Myths, New Realities* (Washington, D.C.: AARP, 1985), 20.

Figure 4.3

EMPLOYMENT APPROACHES FOR RETAINING OLDER WORKERS

All Companies

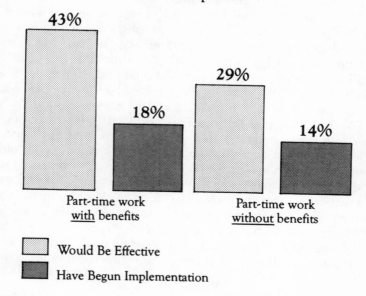

43%

29%

18%

14%

Part-time work
<u>with</u> benefits

Part-time work
<u>without</u> benefits

Would Be Effective

Have Begun Implementation

Source: American Association of Retired Persons. Adapted from *Workers Over 50: Old Myths, New Realities* (Washington, D.C.: AARP, 1985), 20.

Patterns of Discrimination

Most experts, including corporate heads who do offer training to upgrade older workers' skills, believe that the ambivalence in corporate policies stems from the persistent belief that older workers do not *want* additional training and would not respond well even when they were offered it.

Mark Twain once said, "History may not repeat itself, but it rhymes." Current corporate ambiguity in pronouncements and practices regarding older workers has a familiar ring: There is a remarkable similarity between the underlying attitudes about older workers and the beliefs many managers held about female and minority workers 20 years ago. That earlier social and legislative impetus for change in corporate practices; employer resistance in some cases, creative and adaptive management in others; the self-fulfilling prophesies; side battles over statistics, and equity issues vis-à-vis unprotected workers—all have striking parallels in the issues surrounding employment of older employees.

Going against the grain, however, are employers that have adopted specific strategies to employ, upgrade, and retain older workers. Because they represent accomplished fact, these initiatives stand as clear channel markers amidst the swirling tides of speculation about what might, could, or should be done in this critical human resource area. The National Older Workers Information System (NOWIS), formerly operated by the School of Social Work at the University of Michigan and now operated by the American Association of Retired Persons (AARP), has documented 369 programs and practices that provide innovative work options for older employees. These include retiree employment pools, older-worker hiring programs, phased retirement, and training programs.

Of the 180 companies in NOWIS, three-fourths have adopted one or two innovative approaches to older-worker deployment and 10 percent have four or more such programs under way.[7] The NOWIS database includes a range of industry types (see Figure 4.4), of which manufacturing is most prevalent, accounting for 38 percent of the programs. In at least one respect, these are similar

Figure 4.4

INDUSTRIAL MIX IN NOWIS

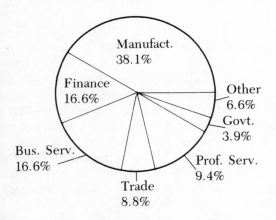

Source: U.S. Congress, Senate Special Committee on Aging, *Personnel Practices for an Aging Work Force: Private-Sector Examples* (Washington, D.C.: Government Printing Office, 1985), 7.

to the other alternative employment strategies discussed in this book: there are multiple factors spurring them, but clear patterns emerge. Chief among those patterns is the recognition of older-worker programs as tools for maximizing profit. In building the NOWIS database, University of Michigan researchers found that although altruistic motives may have stimulated innovative practices helpful to older workers, the practices are continued because they are also advantageous to the company.

Case Histories

The case histories that follow will illustrate how and why corporations are trying to retain and solicit the services of people who, by traditional definition, should have their working careers behind them. The policies and practices presented are only samples.[8] Generally, programs for expanded or more effective employment of older workers fall into several categories, including

- removal of hiring restrictions
- training
- part-time employment
- transitions to retirement

The last category—transitions to retirement—is especially important to the effectiveness of older-worker performance, as opposed to its mere extension in time. Some of the case histories will show how a worker's thoughtful exploration of retirement as an option—without pressure from the employer—tends to produce a decision that is beneficial to both parties.

The case histories will be presented by company, rather than by category of older-worker program. This is because successful company initiatives tend to be integrated, both internally and in regard to other human resource policies and practices. They also tend to reflect a particular management philosophy about work and retirement—one that may have changed over time.

Aerospace Corporation

Aerospace Corporation's experience is an example of how corporate attitudes about older workers can change. Established in 1960, Aerospace is a nonprofit, federally funded research and development center based in Los Angeles, California. It conducts engineering for national security programs, and half of its 4,200 employees are engineers and scientists. The company has never had mandatory retirement (a practice prohibited by California law since 1978). However, at one time it had policies, practices, and incentives that encouraged employees to retire at age 65 or younger.

In 1978, the firm administered a special "early-out" program for professional employees who were vested in the company's retirement plan and who had 10 or more years of service. Under that program, employees could retire with severance pay equal to one week's pay per year of service. In addition, each early retiree received "bridging payments" of $375 per month for 48 months or until age 62, whichever came sooner. The program had a six-month "window" within which eligible employees could opt for participation.

The responses of employees who were offered the early-out program were instructive. Of the 76 who took advantage of it, only about half, or 39, retired. Of the remaining 37, 9 immediately took full-time jobs as engineers at salaries equal to or greater than those they were paid at Aerospace. Another five Aerospace employees became real-estate salesmen, having prepared by taking courses while employed at Aerospace. They used the bridging pay to help get established. Three of the early-outers became educational administrators, and one became a contracting engineer for the state. Twenty went into business for themselves, five of them as licensed building contractors.

In late 1979, the company began studying the feasibility of an ongoing program to help employees prepare for second careers. The study was shelved when an increase in orders made it necessary for Aerospace not only to retain the talent it had, but to hire annuitants. By 1982, the company had 47 regular full-time employees who were age 65 or older; the oldest was a 70-year-old engineer who was hired at age 68.

The company's retirees and near-retirees work under several special arrangements. Some are hired as part-time "casual" employees. Each such employee may work up to 1,000 hours a year while receiving company retirement benefits. Retirees also are hired as consultants. In 1982, Aerospace had 35 consultants whom it, previously had employed as managers, professionals, and administrators. The company sometimes uses retired professionals on special projects. For example, a team of retired managers designed and implemented an employment interview training program for use in recruiting, and a retired executive developed an internal training course in aerospace engineering.

Robert Rubenstein, Aerospace personnel director, observes that the program does more than provide the company continuing access to valuable skills—it denies those skills to competitors. Were it not for the retiree employment program, as the company learned in 1978, "It would be possible for them to leave our company, take our retirement benefits, and go to work for somebody else. That wouldn't make any sense. So why not give them the opportunity to work here?"

The Aerospace employee training programs are consistent with this philosophy. Although there are no special programs for older workers as such, they frequently participate in both management and technical training. The management training prepares engineers and scientists to step up to management under the firm's promote-from-within policy.

The company's retirement plan is likewise geared to the corporate strategy of recruiting and retaining experienced people. The plan has special vesting provisions for older participants. Employees age 55 and over who are terminated due to reduction in force are eligible for accelerated vesting based on their age and length of service. Partial vesting can be earned with as little as one year of service, and full vesting is given any employee age 55 to 65 who is laid off in a reduction in force. All employees, regardless of service, become fully vested at age 65. While ERISA allowed employers to exclude from pension plan participation persons hired within five years of an employer's normal retirement age, Aerospace did not do so. Moreover, employees working beyond age 65 continue to accrue retirement benefit credits.

Bankers Life and Casualty Company

Headquartered in Chicago, Bankers Life has assets in excess of $1 billion and ranks in the top 2 percent of insurance companies. It has a home-office work force of 2,700 and employs 2,000 people in the field. Like Aerospace Corporation, the company has never had a mandatory retirement age; about 3 percent of its home-office workers are over 65, and they receive the same employee benefits and pension accruals as their fellow employees. Bankers Life maintains age-neutral practices in all other aspects of human resource management, including employment, training, and development. It has traditionally hired individuals over age 50.

The company's approach to personal planning services for employees is noteworthy. Bankers Life offers employee seminars and other educational programs on such subjects as retirement planning, legal matters, investments, and second-career development. The firm no longer calls this "preretirement planning," however. In testimony before the Senate Special Committee on Aging, a spokesman explained, "When you are 55 and you have 10 years to go, and somebody tells you how to invest your funds, you don't have that much room left. So we have changed it [preretirement planning] to life planning."[9] It is available to employees of all ages.

An employee who is anticipating retirement is encouraged to register with the human resources department for a combination of phased retirement, flexible work schedules, and part-time work. One postretirement option is participation in a temporary worker pool formed in 1979, through which annuitants may work full- or part-time temporary schedules. The retiree-temp arrangement got off to a fast start when, at 8:00 a.m. on the first day of the program, a manager requested the immediate assistance of six retirees. They were on the job within an hour. The manager estimated that the annuitants would complete the project in eight hours; they finished in less than three. Word spread quickly, and requests for the retirees began pouring in. By the end of the first year, the program had eliminated the need for THS firm employees, saving Bankers Life over $10,000 in fees. Also eliminated was the expense of orienting temporary employees unfamiliar with company procedures.

The company considers the retiree pool extremely effective, estimating the cost of filling jobs with experienced retirees to be one third that of using alternative means. Today, about 50 people are registered for pool assignments, with 15 to 20 at work during busy periods. They fill primarily clerical jobs at an average wage of $5 per hour. These employees receive no employee benefits, but they retain their annuitant health-care coverage.

A Bankers Life spokesman summed up the company's philosophy and experience as follows:

> It would have been difficult for someone to try to convince our managers that an employee who was perfectly adequate on December 18 was suddenly not capable of doing the job any longer on December 19 just because he or she became age 65. It didn't make any sense then, and it certainly doesn't make any sense now.[10]

Polaroid Corporation

This manufacturer of instant cameras, film, and related equipment is headquartered in Cambridge, Massachusetts, and employees 11,000 people in the United States. Annual sales exceed $1.3 billion. Polaroid has several programs to retain the expertise of experienced employees and to smooth the transition for those who wish to retire. The company has never had a fixed, mandatory retirement age. In the 1950s, it operated an extension review program through which employees could request approval to work beyond age 65; the majority of those requests were approved. Upon amendment of ADEA in 1978, the system was changed to apply to employees age 70 and over. Polaroid employees who continue to work past age 65 maintain full benefits, including pension credits and profit sharing. The firm permits retirement as early as age 55, with pensions discounted by 3 percent per year for those retiring early.

The firm's retirement benefits include a profit-sharing plan, pension plan, and family medical and life insurance benefits. Polaroid estimates that an employee who retires at age 65 after 30 years of service may expect retirement income of from 60 to 65 percent of preretirement salary. That estimate is based on a combination of company pension, Social Security, and profit sharing. Of the 1,700 employees who have retired under Polaroid's flexible system, about 60 percent retired before age 65, 20 percent at 65, and 20 percent after 65.

The firm offers a variety of options to help potential retirees make the best decision. One popular plan is rehearsal retirement, under which potential retirees may take unpaid leaves of up to six months to gauge their reactions to a prolonged separation from work. The average leave is three months. To be eligible for rehearsal retirement, an employee must be at least age 55 and have one full year of service. During the leave, the employee accrues no benefits, but may continue group insurance coverage by paying the premiums. Polaroid admits that lack of pay for the employee during rehearsal retirement and the difficulty of finding a temporary replacement are possible drawbacks. But management is obviously pleased with the net effect: Of those who have tried rehearsal retirement, half have returned to work on a full-time basis.[11]

"Tapering-off" schedules provide a gradual transition to retirement at the company. Under this program, an employee's schedule of hours per day, days per week, or weeks per month may be reduced over a period as long as three to five years. The specifics are negotiated in each case between employee and supervisor. It is understood in all cases that flexibility may be required. Workers on a tapering-off plan are paid only for hours worked; if they work more than 1,000 hours per year, most benefits are prorated. All employees on tapering-off schedules receive full medical insurance and prorated pension credits.

Polaroid also provides several postretirement employment options. Annuitants may be hired as contract consultants; these are usually engineers and technical employees. Other retirees may be hired on a per-diem basis through an independent employment agency; the company also administers a retiree temp pool similar to the one at Bankers Life. All the options are presented to employees in a series of preretirement counseling sessions and presentations.

Grumman Corp.

A large aerospace firm, Grumman employs over 32,000 people; about 21,000 of them working at the corporation's headquarters and plants in Bethpage, New York. The Bethpage staff is complemented by 1,150 "job shoppers," who work on an as-needed basis. A number of the "shoppers" are Grumman retirees. Dan Knowles, Grumman vice president for personnel and administration, first surveyed retirees 15 years ago to gauge their interest in returning to work in some capacity. More than 50 percent responded positively. Today, about 150 Grumman retirees work at Bethpage on any given day.

The Grumman cadre is different from the on-call annuitant pools of many other firms in two respects. First, it includes a higher percentage of professionals. Second, Grumman's pension plan prohibits retirees from working directly for the firm, so they are hired as independent contractors through an outside agency that handles payroll and related administrative tasks. These workers—especially the engineers—are paid higher cash compensation than regular employees performing similar jobs; however, they receive none of the benefits provided regular employees.

Grumman calls on its retirees in several ways. In some cases, a manager requests a particular person to work on a project for several months. In other situations, retirees are called in to conduct training classes or to work one-on-one with inexperienced engineers. Ready availability of these experienced employees has proved a valuable resource to Grumman. But there is another reason why the firm uses retirees and other contract personnel: Between 1969 and 1977, Grumman laid off 13,000 workers. The current pool of job shoppers is designed in part to provide a buffer against future reductions in the core work force. When production orders fall off, overtime is eliminated, and contract employees are let go before regular employees. The plan seems to be working effectively. According to Knowles, the number of job shoppers at Bethpage fluctuated by more than 200 between July 1985 and July 1986, while only a handful of regular employees were laid off during that period.

Johnson and Johnson Products

Headquartered in New Brunswick, New Jersey, this firm permits retirees to work as temporary employees for up to 40 hours a month while drawing pension benefits. Like Grumman and others, Johnson and Johnson has trimmed its work force in recent years, and it regularly budgets for temporaries as a buffer to protect the remaining core of regular employees.

Johnson and Johnson has found that as some professionals retire, ancillary functions of their jobs may be broken off and spread among other employees, leaving only the central tasks (a common practice in today's environment of lean staffing). If the core duties of a retiring employee require only five hours a day to complete and the company needs a specialist to concentrate exclusively on them, says a company spokesman, "[the] first logical thought has got to be that [retiring] employee. Bringing him or her back in that position makes a lot of sense. [Retirees] are bringing back tons of experience. They know the organization and have a sense of what we're doing." Although the company also relies on agency temps, the preference of managers who have temporary vacancies is clearly in favor of the Johnson and Johnson annuitants.

Stouffer Foods Corporation

Most of the older men and women involved in the programs described thus far have been white-collar workers. Can the human resource potential of older workers also be maximized in an assembly-line environment? In 1978, Stouffer Foods formed a task force to answer that question.

A subsidiary of the Nestle Company, Stouffer manufactures food products for retail and institutional customers. It employs 4,000 of whom 1,800 work at its frozen food plant in Solon, Ohio. The Solon plant has two types of product (assembly) lines: the retail lines, which assemble small packages for retail stores; and the institutional lines, which assemble larger packages for customers such as cafeterias and hospitals. Because the institutional lines involve more manual handling, they are slower paced.

In cooperation with an exercise physiologist from Michigan State University, Stouffer began a project under which workers were tested for muscle strength on a Cybex II machine. Initially, approximately 100 employees participated, and from the data gathered on them, Stouffer established baseline strength requirements for various jobs in the plant. More than 1,000 workers have now participated. When employees experiencing physical problems on the job are tested, the results help the company determine whether exercise, retraining, or transfer to another job is necessary. The Cybex test is also used in pre-employment screening and to evaluate the capabilities of employees bidding for certain jobs. The company emphasizes that the Cybex program is not designed as a "weeding-out" tool. An exercise physiologist recommends physical conditioning programs for employees who wish to increase their strength and flexibility. A number of employees have taken advantage of this option and rebid successfully for higher-level jobs.

Based in part on the Cybex evaluation, some older workers who are having difficulty with the work on the retail lines, especially in cases in which safety may be a factor, are gradually shifted to the slower-paced lines, where their abilities are effectively employed. The slower-paced lines are part of a two-shift operation, each with a complement of approximately 25 workers. More than half of the employees on these lines are over age 45, one of them a 72-year-old woman. Stouffer employees earn in excess of $10 per hour and receive regular benefits, including medical and dental insurance. The firm also hires older workers and retirees for part-time work on a call-in basis. Part-time and temporary employees receive prorated vacations and holidays, but no other benefits. The company has a preretirement tapering-off program, and about 10 percent of eligible employees take advantage of it.

Re-Employment of Retirees as an Unintended Consequence

For some companies, re-enlistment of retired professionals has been the antithesis of a planned strategy. DuPont is one such firm. In 1985, the Wilmington, Delaware-based conglomerate designed a voluntary early retirement program to thin the ranks. DuPont estimated that 6,000 employees would opt for the program, which featured enhanced early retirement benefits. Instead, 11,500 employees took advantage of the package, forcing the company to bring back several thousand as consultants for up to a year.[12]

What Can Be Learned From Successful Older-Worker Programs

The successful human resource strategies outlined in the previous section show that management need not be confounded by either the data concerning older-worker preferences and availability or the conflicting interpretations of well-informed experts. They represent accomplishments achieved both *because of* and *in spite of* economic, social, and legislative changes. Companies that have not hampered themselves with arbitrary restrictions on the potential of seasoned workers are far better positioned to deal with future changes in the external environment. Especially given the recent major changes in age-discrimination and pension legislation, the remark of an Atlantic Richfield spokesman in 1980 was prophetic: "Companies that look at their work force more as self-responsible individuals with choices to make and that have a company philosophy to provide opportunities for those choices, are further down the road on this question of working beyond age 65."[13]

Certainly, the case histories show that employing older workers represents a good deal more than the well-publicized "McDonald's syndrome"—a problem facing the fast-food industry, where chains are forced to hire older people because teenagers are unwilling to take, or are unavailable for, low-paying jobs.

Persistent Myths About Older Workers

Why, then, have so few companies sought to increase rather than cut short the potential of mature workers? The greatest impediment to effective deployment of older workers is management's belief that aging is synonymous with declining health, safety, productivity, and motivation. A Sun Oil Company spokesman relates that when Sun adopted a program to call in retirees for temporary jobs some managers were afraid of having "little old ladies and men tottering around." The "little-old-lady" mind-set is comprised of several related myths about older workers that have been instilled in many of us and reinforced in much the same way as were old stereotypes about the work ethic and abilities of minorities and women in nontraditional roles. Rejection of the older-worker myths is at least implied in the corporate strategies reviewed earlier. The experiences of those and other companies with regard to the true capabilities of older workers are consistent with the results of independent research. Some of the popular myths dispelled by their findings are outlined in the following paragraphs.

Unreliability

This notion holds that workers become less reliable as they grow older. Reliability is usually defined in terms of attendance, turnover, and safety. The idea that older workers perform poorly in these areas is based on the thesis that older workers have relatively poor health and attention spans and that, lacking the career drive of younger workers, they are inclined to stay home with even minor aches and pains. However, Polaroid Corporation, which closely monitors employee attendance, has concluded: "We have never seen any data to support the myth that older employees are ill and absent more often than other employees." In fact, 18 percent of its age-65-and-over employees have perfect attendance, versus 10 percent for the total work force.[14]

Banker's Life has also found that older employees have attendance records at least equal to those of younger employees. An internal study showed that 34 of 128 over-age-65 employees studied (26.6 percent) had perfect attendance; only 13 of 128 employees under age 65 (10.2 percent) had perfect attendance. Although absences for the over-65 group tended to be for slightly longer periods, they were less frequent. It is also significant that there were twice as many half-day absences in the under-65 Bankers Life group than in the older group. Most managers agree that half-day, "Friday flu," and other casual absences play far more havoc with work scheduling and quality control than do long-term absences. The Bankers Life experience is consistent with research data compiled by Richard Johnson, Director of the Florida State Department of Education. He notes that although older workers tend to have longer absences, they are not, on the average, absent any more than younger workers.[15]

According to Glenn Northrup of the American Association of Retired People, employees over age 55 take less time off and are less accident-prone than younger workers. Their illness frequency rate is 1 percent, versus a national rate for all workers of 3.1 percent. Although there are slight variations from study to study, internal company surveys, supervisory ratings, and independent investigations all confirm that older workers' attendance is at least equal to that of their younger co-workers.

While older workers are more susceptible to certain types of accidents such as falls and being hit by flying objects, their safety performance generally exceeds that of younger groups. A Bureau of Labor Statistics study of workers' compensation data concluded that occupational injuries are more frequent among younger employees. Workers age 20 to 24 have the highest injury rate; rates then drop off with increased age, and the drop is sharpest for the over-65-age category.[16] However, other research has found that once injured, older workers take longer to recuperate and that they are more likely to suffer permanent disability or die from accidents.[17]

The low overall accident frequency rate of senior employees is especially remarkable considering that in 1981, 25 percent of workers age 65 and over were employed in agriculture, mining, construction, and manufacturing. Since continued growth is expected in the service sector—now the source of nine out of ten new jobs—while there will be continued declines in agricultural and manufacturing employment, older workers' already good safety record should improve. Whatever the future holds, employers who have adopted prudent programs to maximize the skills of older workers have found no cause for concern with respect to job safety. On the contrary, they are pleased with the safety record of their senior employees.

Turnover rates of older workers are decidedly lower than those of younger employees. Firms such as Western Savings and Loan of Arizona and First Savings of San Diego regularly hire older tellers specifically for that reason. AARP data show that employees age 20 to 30 stay with a company an average of only 3.4 years; those age 50 to 60 remain for an average of 15. Similar data from the U.S. Department of Labor confirm the higher mobility of younger employees. Workers typically hold about 10 jobs over a lifetime. (Chapters 6 and 7 will deal with some of the reasons why the mobility of today's and tomorrow's young workers will be even greater.)

Finally, it should be noted that many retirements are classified as due to health reasons. Parnes found that 51 percent of some 2,000 men who retired between 1966 and 1976 attributed their decisions to poor health.[18] Does this contradict the picture of older workers as relatively healthy and reliable? Several explanations suggest that it does not. First, it is difficult to sort out health from economic and other personal factors that affect the retirement decision. Parnes noted that the statements "My health was bad," "I was tired of working," and "I had a good pension" could all describe the retirement decision of an arthritic person with a dull job covered by a liberal pension plan.[19] Among older workers with a strong work ethic, poor health is a relatively acceptable excuse for stepping down. It should also be noted that (among men) retirement for health reasons is concentrated among agricultural and construction workers. There is a general correlation between health-related retirement decisions and relatively low levels of education and socioeconomic status.

Insurance Costs

Some employers believe that older workers represent significantly higher group insurance costs. With regard to hospital and medical costs, a survey of 400 companies conducted by Yankelovich, Skelly, and White, Inc., found that 37 percent of the firms surveyed perceived health insurance to be extremely or very costly for a 30-year-old female with two dependents and 32 percent perceived it to be so for a 30-year-old male with two dependents. By comparison, 30 and 29 percent perceived health insurance as costly for 65-year-old male and female retirees, respectively. However, only 16 and 15 percent perceived it to be so with regard to 55-year-old females and males.[20] Sixty-two percent of respondents said that the extra cost of health insurance coverage for older employees was insignificant compared to total company health care costs.

Bankers Life reports that, because of Medicare coverage, the cost of insuring older workers actually has decreased under noncompulsory retirement. They have also found that concerns other employers may have about skyrocketing long-term disability insurance are not warranted. The company notes that only the healthiest older workers—those unlikely to become disabled—tend to stay on past normal retirement age.[21]

Overall Employment Costs

The belief that older workers cost more to employ in terms of overall costs is based in part on that fact that senior employees tend to be in higher pay grades and in higher ranges within grades.

But this truism answers the wrong question. Results-oriented managers do not ask, 'What is the (human) asset's cost?" They ask, "What is the asset's net contribution to organizational goals?" The Yankelovich, Skelly, and White researchers took that perspective in their survey by asking respondents whether "the cost of older workers is justified when you consider value to the company." Ninety percent responded favorably.

Because turnover is so much lower among older employees, the high costs of recruiting and training replacements are likewise reduced. In focus-group sessions with employers, AARP has found that companies often forget to factor in these costs when they consider the relative merits of retaining older workers. Firms that have adopted strategies to retain the skills of experienced workers also point out that when an employee retires and is replaced, the employer is essentially paying two people: the annuitant, who receives pension payments and perhaps annuitant health care and life insurance benefits, and the replacement, who receives a salary and full employee benefits.

With regard to the cost of continuing pension accruals for employees who work beyond age 65, one major study concluded that as the number of workers over age 65 increases, employer pension costs will *decline* because the costs of continued contributions and crediting will be more than offset by gains from the shortened duration of pension payments. For example, the study determined that, should post-65 employment increase by 25 percent, employer costs would decline by $16.9 million by year 5 and even more in later years. If post-65 employment should increase by 50 percent, employers would realize annual pension *savings* of more than $600 million by year 15, despite the cost of post-65 contributions and crediting.[22]

Atlantic Richfield is one company that has rejected the claim that older individuals are relatively expensive to employ. This major petroleum company, which had 54,000 employees in 1980, eliminated mandatory retirement in 1978. (Although the firm is based in California, where mandatory retirement was outlawed that year, its decision applied nationwide.) Ending mandatory retirement was but part of a major policy decision to eliminate disincentives for mature employees to continue working. The company began providing workers who stayed beyond age 65 the same benefits as other employees, including group medical and life insurance, a thrift plan, an employee stock ownership plan (ESOP), and long-term disability coverage to age 69.

The firm also continues pension accruals for employees over age 65 and permits them to continue voluntary supplemental pension contributions. The pension formula is based on final average salary. Atlantic Richfield has described the move as a sound, cost-effective approach, one that "creates one class of employee and not a dual classification. . . . We think it is very helpful."[23] The company also abolished a policy that prohibited re-employment of its annuitants and began rehiring them, as needed, in the same manner as new employees. They receive regular employee benefits while continuing to draw their pensions, in effect "double-dipping." In fact, these individuals increase their pension benefit levels through continued employment. Although primarily aimed at people who have critical skills in the earth and computer sciences, the program applies companywide.[24]

Not every company needs to go, nor can it go, as far as Atlantic Richfield in providing incentives for experienced staff to stay on. But it is clear that a number of profit-minded firms have found that older employees pay their way in terms of net value added to the organization.

Performance Deterioration

Everyone ages, and with aging comes inevitable change. Some employers conclude from this fact that the older employee is bound to start losing mental and physical work capacity. Yet the natural aging process has not been a major problem to companies that encourage longer work force participation. There are several reasons:

- First, the myth somewhat begs the question. Research demonstrates that chronological age is an increasingly poor predictor of physical or mental ability.
- Declines that are associated with aging—whether aging begins at age 30 or age 80—are not necessarily relevant to job performance. Johnson and Riker have pointed out that most employees are working well within their physical and mental limits, and therefore suffer no performance declines as a result of the aging process. They conclude that the slight changes that occur "cannot be used as excuses by either employers or employees to explain a poor performance record."[25]
- These observations are borne out by, among many others, Department of Labor (DOL) studies published in 1965 that

found only a slight decline in productivity among age-45-and-over factory workers doing substantial physical labor. Among office workers, the group aged 65 and over had the best performance record; for mail sorters, production remained stable up to age 60.[26]

- A 1977 Senate report reviewed DOL studies made in the 1950s of 3,000 retail, industrial, office, and managerial workers age 60 and over. Most of them performed as well as or better than younger workers on measures of quality and quantity of work.[27]

The perception that aging means "going downhill" persists mainly because it is the sparkplug for a self-fulfilling prophesy. When employees approach an arbitrary retirement age, they and their supervisors often slip into what Polaroid vice president of personnel Harold Page refers to as "an unspoken ease-off contract" under which fewer demands are placed on them. This signals to employees that management expects them to retire and is making plans that assume their cooperation. Among other things, in return for a lighter workload, management expects them not to take new initiatives, not to take up training slots in an attempt to keep skills current, and certainly not to talk about working beyond retirement age. Employees who have 20 or so years of service invested find little reason to rock the boat. (This is true at least while they are employed. However, this employer strategy can backfire in the form of postretirement age-discrimination suits.)

As "Old Charlie's" office or shopmates see him taking it easy, they naturally assume that it is because he is getting up in years. They may well conclude that a beneficent management is showing compassion by "feathering him back." Thus, he seems to confirm that older workers quickly decline in usefulness, know it, and are grateful to be allowed to coast until mercifully "put out to pasture." The premise thus fulfilled, rationalization of the company's retirement policy—whether the policy is written or understood—is now complete.

The "ease-off contract" is also useful to managers who are uncomfortable setting tough performance standards for and appraising workers who might be their parents' age. And it is heartily welcomed by the truly mediocre "Old Charlies." As suggested by much of the data presented in this chapter, the real loser in this situation is the corporation.

Suppose that the performance of a 72-year-old employee does start to slip, perhaps because of gradual memory loss and a decline in attention span. How is this handled by companies that do not encourage older workers to leave at normal retirement age or earlier? Their answer is uniform: "We don't—the employee does." Testifying before the Senate Special Committee on Aging, a Bankers Life spokesman reported that in the company's 40-year history, no manager could recall having to sit down with an older worker and suggest it was time to retire. He explained, "Those who have chosen to stay beyond retirement have far more self-discipline than any manager would ever give them, and when they feel they are slipping, they go to the boss and say, 'I think I would like to plan on retiring.' "[28]

The Training Investment

It is often held that it generally is not a good investment to train or retrain older workers. This belief has three related rationales: (1) Most older workers are not interested in training to upgrade their skills or to prepare for career advancement; (2) even when they attempt to learn new skills or technologies, they do not learn as fast or as well as younger people; (3) there is little point training workers who can be expected to retire within 5 to 10 years because young employees with many years of service ahead offer a much better return on the training-and-development dollar.

The first point is often thought of in terms of training intended to help prepare employees for advancement. Robert L. Craig, former president of the American Society for Training and Development, has found that employees age 50 and over are least likely to seek new training. "They just seem to lose some of their ambition," he concludes. David Gamse, director of AARP's Worker Equity Program replies:

> We have a self-fulfilling prophesy. Today's older workers are of a generation that was taught from day one that you can't teach an old dog new tricks . . . you have to make way for the incoming generation. They've been conditioned to believe that they have to get out because they are not capable of learning.

Management often reinforces this negative self-image through retirement and promotion practices. As employers have learned from affirmative action efforts, it takes more than pronouncements and neutral policies to overcome the effects of this sort of life-long conditioning. Gamse concludes that with respect to older workers, industry is about where it was 15 years ago with women and minorities. But, as with apparent race and sex discrimination, the problem does not necessarily lie with either management or employee; there is only so much room for advancement in an organization. Some career specialists estimate that less than 1 percent of the people in an organization make it to the top decision-making level. Considering the substantial increase expected in the number of middle-age managers in coming decades, employees seeking to move up will find the organizational triangle beginning to narrow at ever-lower levels. As noted by Senator John Heinz, chairman of the Senate Special Committee on Aging, "We've always defined career advancement as a linear process, so if you're not moving upward you're a failure."[29] The belief that older workers are not interested in promotion is thus another partial truth that responds to the wrong question. At the conclusion of this chapter, redefining success will be discussed as a key element in effective programs for older workers.

Of course there are other reasons for training and retraining than simply as preparation for advancement. With technology changing so rapidly, employees in many fields must be retrained continually just to keep up. Technical recruiters, educators, and managers agree that the "half-life" of an individual's technical knowledge, that is, the time required for 50 percent of it to become obsolete, is becoming shorter and shorter.

In both management and technical training, major companies have put the older-worker-as-poor-trainee myth to the test. General Electric's Aerospace Electronic Systems Department in Utica, New York, is a useful example because it speaks to both the trainability of mature professionals and the effects of successful training on posttraining behavior. The department designs and develops electronics for missiles, aircraft, and space vehicles. It employs 3,000 people, of whom 900 are in engineering.

In 1977 the department developed a "Technical Renewal Program" for long-service engineers whose skills had become outdated due to a dramatic switch to digital design technology in the industry. The program was consistent with the company's policy of continuing education for employees. During the program's three years of operation, 235 engineers were selected by their managers to participate. The average age of these participants was 45, and they averaged almost 20 years of company service. Some of them took as many as two or three of the nine courses offered; some of the advanced courses were the equivalent of 3 college credits, running 12 weeks in length. Participants spent half the workday in class and half at their regular jobs. Only a few of the participants failed to complete the program.

A follow-up study showed that more than 70 percent of the participants who did complete the courses were immediately moved to new assignments in new project areas. Even those who did not apply the new skills in their positions were able to interact more effectively with others because of the information they had gathered in the course. Some of the participants have since been promoted, although not as a direct result of the training. Many of the participants who were initially resistant to retraining were pleased with the courses.

The Technical Renewal Program ended in 1980 when the immediate need for concentrated training had been met, but the department operates a continuing in-house engineering education program. It offers new courses every year on an after-hours basis. As of 1982, about 50 percent of the older engineers who participated in the original program had continued on their own initiative to take the courses offered under the continuing program. Since 1977, when 150 to 200 employees participated in 10 to 15 courses a semester, the program has grown to 700 participants and 28 courses a semester. With projections indicating that 42 percent of the engineering professional staff will reach normal retirement age (age 62) within the next 10 years, efforts are under way to develop a skills-retention program in which key employees develop and conduct courses and work with younger engineers to assure vital skill and technology transfer. The company estimates that it would cost three times as much to hire fresh graduates schooled in the latest technology, not to mention the possibility that they would have to be laid off if business declined.

At Grumman, nearly 60 percent of the employees participating in a retraining program to develop systems engineers are over age 40. Dan Knowles, vice president for personnel and administration, has found that in addition to the direct costs of recruitment and orientation, "you need three career-development analysts to steady a youngster just out of school."[30]

Are there differences in learning styles and efficiency between older and younger trainees? Johnson and Riker found that, in general, younger workers seem to respond more quickly in the first phases of training, but mature workers catch up quickly and, in many cases, surpass them. One oil company tested 100 workers at the conclusion of 120 hours of retraining and found that the older workers earned better final grades.[31]

In a study of the literature on employee responses to different training methods, Doering, Rhodes, and Schuster found evidence that older workers tend to learn as well as younger ones—except when stress is applied. This is not surprising. If older workers come to the training room conditioned to believe that they may look foolish competing with young people who are much more recently out of school, a high-stress training situation may indeed bring about that result. Where older workers were given self-paced, programmed instruction, however, the researchers found that they tended to learn at least as well as younger trainees.[32]

The results of tests conducted both in the United States and abroad were summarized by Johnson and Riker as follows:

> Mature persons do better than younger ones on tests requiring pre-planning and making certain kinds of decisions. Apparently the wisdom gathered through experience pays off in enabling mature persons to evaluate tasks and project outcomes more accurately.
>
> Intelligence, as measured by I.Q. tests, remains virtually constant over the life cycle. Intellectual abilities associated with creativity, such as ability to create ideas, express oneself, and work freely with ideas, seem to increase with age. . . . The evidence is contrary to the myth, "You can't teach an old dog new tricks."[33]

The evidence shows further that older workers are more likely to complete their training and to remain longer with their employers thereafter. Indeed, how many times have managers lamented the job-hopping of younger employees thus: "We train people so they can go out and get better jobs with our competitors"?

The Flexibility Question

It is a common belief that older workers are less flexible than younger workers in adapting to change. To the extent that this assertion implies that older workers simply do not have the cognitive tools to understand and assimilate new concepts and technology, the evidence cited with respect to training clearly negates it. More often, however, "less flexible" refers to resistance to change. Yankelovich, Skelly, and White found this to be one of the more troublesome areas reported in their survey of company CEOs and human resources executives. Companies with 1,000 or more employees seemed particularly concerned; 48 percent of them perceived technology as important to the future of their organizations, but only 11 percent rated older workers as excellent or very good in terms of "comfort with new technologies" (see Figure 4.5). There are several possible explanations.

Figure 4.5

COMFORT WITH NEW TECHNOLOGIES

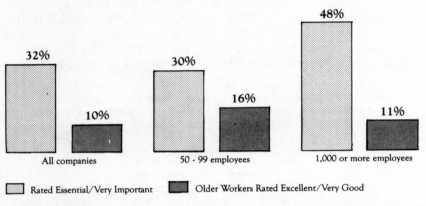

Rated Essential/Very Important   Older Workers Rated Excellent/Very Good

Source: American Association of Retired Persons. Adapted from *Workers Over 50: Old Myths, New Realities* (Washington, D.C.: AARP, 1985), 13.

First, the only area in which the surveyed firms perceived older workers somewhat negatively is the one least subject to confirmation. Unlike performance measures such as quality and quantity of work, the perception of an employee subgroup's "comfort with new ideas" is subjective. It is difficult to imagine a group of employees who are generally applauded as loyal, highly motivated, superior performers, who, nonetheless, tend not to respond well when management tries to introduce new and better ways of doing things.

It may be that the image of the mature worker as uneasy with new ideas is simply a tool for confirming our cultural predisposition that the old must make way for the young. Such a phenomenon is not new. Many managers and supervisors once rationalized that women would not be "comfortable" in men's jobs and that clients would not be comfortable if called on by a woman or a black.

Yankelovich and others have suggested that older workers' lack of "comfort" with new ideas may in fact be a sign of a healthy skepticism because they have seen many technological panaceas fail. In the field of management, especially, seasoned employees have cause for skepticism about "new" techniques. Those who have been in the work force for a few decades will recall such "breakthroughs" as Quality Assurance, Zero Defects, Quality Circles, Centralization-Decentralization (and back again), Management by Objectives (MBO), Material Requirements Planning (MRP), Short Interval Planning (SIS), "One-Minute" Management, Management by Walking Around, "Excellent" Management, Transactional Analysis, Value Analysis, Zero-Based Budgeting, Zero Inventory, T-groups, G-groups, X-Y Management, Z-management, EST, and Portfolio Analysis.[34]

The surviving seniors at an aerospace firm will not soon forget the productivity improvement program the company began some years ago. Launched with fanfare, it was called "PRIDE." Whatever that acronym originally signified, major staff cuts soon caused employees to conclude that it truly meant "Prepare Résumé Immediately: Department Eliminated."

In a cover story on business fads, *Business Week* quoted a marketing manager as follows: "In the past 18 months, we have heard that profit is more important than revenue, that quality is more important than profit, that people are more important than profit, that customers are more important than our people, that big customers are more important than small customers, and that growth is the key to our success. No wonder our performance is inconsistent."[35]

That *Business Week* story, published in January 1986, noted "intrapreneurship" as "in." By August, *The New York Times* described that much-heralded corporate fad as "fading fast."[36] While many of these ideas are based on sound principle, they are often hastily implemented, then abandoned, by revolving-door managers in search of a quick solution to deeply embedded problems. In many cases, then, the long-term employee's lack of enthusiasm for the newest program simply reflects his or her experience with management's penchant for latching on to the latest fads.

The major corporations that have sought to make use of the experience of senior employees in new situations have found them to be neither reticent nor inflexible. IBM concluded that employees over age 45 were *more* flexible than younger ones in conforming to job changes.[37]

Advancement Opportunities for Younger Workers

Some companies fear that if they do not encourage older employees to retire the organization will become top-heavy with them. In contrast, firms that have not had mandatory retirement and that, indeed, have hired people who were forcibly retired by other companies, report no such experience. At Bankers Life, the proportion of employees over age 65 has never exceeded 4 percent of the home-office staff or 6.8 percent of the field staff. Most of the company's senior employees retire voluntarily at age 75. As mentioned earlier in this chapter, 23 percent of Polaroid employees remain on the job beyond age 65; but the firm obviously considers their presence an asset, not a liability.

Thus, the evidence dispels the myths about older workers. Both corporate experiences and independent research have shown mature workers to be valuable human resources within organizations that have sought to maximize their potential. Companies that have taken steps to capitalize on the skills and experience of senior workers cite them as more productive than younger workers by virtually every accepted measure.

It has also been shown how myths and stereotypes restrict otherwise astute employers from realizing the competitive edge of older workers. Those impediments are similar to the ones that for many years blocked, and in some cases still block, full realization of human potential because of race, sex, or religion. But the pattern with regard to older workers is different in one notable respect: Once negative stereotypes of minorities and of the sexes are dispelled, it becomes clear that there is no inherent difference in job performance between ethnic groups or the sexes. Ironically, when the stereotypes about *older workers* are put aside, management finds that they are not only superior performers, but superior in the very qualities that the stereotypes suggest they lack.

Key Elements for Successful Deployment of Older Workers

Although employers use different programs to maximize the talents of mature workers, there are several common, critical elements.

Employee Selection and Performance Standards

Experienced human resource managers and attorneys know that unsatisfactory employment relationships often involve employees who should never have been hired or placed in their particular positions. A cursory review of the record often shows that such employees could and should have been dealt with years before events gave rise to litigation or some other form of contention. It is not uncommon for a union representative, an arbitrator, or even a compliance agency investigator to say to a personnel manager (off the record and after the dispute is settled) "We could never figure out why you hired that joker in the first place!"

Companies with productive older workers tend not to make such mistakes; they know that poor performance does not commence on the employee's 65th birthday. Xerox Corporation's chief executive officer, Peter McCulough (former chairman of the President's Commission on Pension Policy), believes that performance problems typically show up in an employee's first three years. He directs that new employees be screened and monitored very carefully during that period and that "if there is any question about their performance or their attitude, they should be let go."[38] Bankers Life sets performance standards for all jobs, with productivity being the major guideline; performance is appraised formally every six months.

To make a performance appraisal system work, managers and supervisors must be solidly grounded in the basics of performance standard-setting and appraisal. Just as they must learn to avoid common rating errors such as the halo effect (giving overall ratings—good or bad—on one aspect of the job) or central tendency (rating nearly everyone in a group as average), they should understand the pitfalls of managing older workers. Those include the following:

- The myths about older workers and how both management and employees can unconsciously reinforce them.
- The temptation of the "ease-off" contract, especially when it is consistent with both the employee's and the supervisor's predisposed notions about older workers.
- The tendency of some young managers to avoid criticizing or counseling a subordinate who "could be my mom or dad."

- The inability to deal constructively with the older subordinate who may act paternalistic or condescending toward a young supervisor.
- The temptation to "clean house" by abruptly beginning to document poor performance (real or otherwise) where none has been recorded in the employee's long history with the company.

"Win-Win" Outcomes in Retirement Decisions

What about the *quality* of employees who stay and of those who retire? Might flexible retirement options encourage the right people to leave and the wrong people to stay? Companies that provide such options have found just the opposite; their programs lead to a mutually satisfactory self-selection. Polaroid's comments are typical:

> Overwhelmingly, we find that the people who choose to stay beyond 65 are the people management would choose to have stay. The people that leave early usually have health or performance problems, or their contribution is being diminished in some way. Self-selection is doing exactly what we want it to do."[39]

Even firms that formerly required retirement at age 70 (including some of the NOWIS companies) report that smoothing the transition to retirement has paid off. Now that Congress has outlawed mandatory retirement, programs that lead to "win-win" retirement decisions such as those at Polaroid have even greater significance. The practices outlined in the brief summary that follows show that positive outcomes do not occur by chance. Nor will they materialize through a management policy of simple neutrality or by legislation.

Win-win retirement outcomes flow from the premise that good personal decisions, like good management decisions, are based on good information. The maturing worker has major life choices to make, of which retirement is only one; and related to the retirement decision are both alternative and complementary decisions, options, and opportunities. Forward-thinking employers help employees identify and sort out these choices. The concept of preretirement counseling is not new. But under the traditional approach, it is simply a form of outplacement: An employee nearing normal retirement age sits down with an employee-benefits administrator to review pension calculations and related administrative procedures. The benefits administrator might provide a brochure or two on Social Security and other "things to think about." Some companies take a more elaborate approach, providing formal, group presentations and outside speakers on such subjects as health care, insurance, and financial planning; but the emphasis is still on the *how-to* of retirement rather than on *whether* or *when* to retire.

Companies that take the nontraditional approach to management of older workers do offer information on Medicare, financial planning, and travel to potential retirees, but they also tend to offer broader "life planning" information such as self-assessment and career-change strategies. This is provided to employees well before they near retirement age. The following paragraphs describe a few examples of company programs designed to go even a step beyond.

Control Data Corporation of Minneapolis offers fully paid social service leaves of up to one year to full-time employees who have at least two years of service. A number of older employees who have taken advantage of the program to work for nonprofit community organizations have remained with them as permanent employees or have started their own such organizations.

Pitney Bowes of Stamford, Connecticut, offers retirement educational assistance to all employees over age 50 and their spouses. It covers tuition of $300 per year each for employee and spouse, up to a $3,000 maximum, and continuing for two years after retirement. The program is quite popular and has led a number of employees to profitable second careers and enhanced income after retirement. IBM has had similar results with a similar program.

Some companies in southern California engage the services of The Second Careers Program (SCP) of Los Angeles, a nonprofit agency sponsored by the Los Angeles Voluntary Action Center. SCP designs preretirement programs for companies, focusing on second-career opportunities in areas such as paid employment, self-employment, education, and voluntary service. SCP then makes available to employers, on a fee basis, retirees whom they have helped to establish second-career capabilities.

Expanded Career Options

Senator Heinz's observation that one who is no longer moving up in an organization is often considered a failure was mentioned earlier in this chapter. It is ironic that managements that have strict policies against race-baiting or sexist language in the workplace still use terms such as "deadwood" fairly openly in referring to workers who are not expected to advance further with the company. Such terms are fully as demeaning and debilitating as any racial slur. Employees who need a respite after so many years in high-pressure or physically demanding jobs have an even greater dilemma. Philip Hodges, manager of corporate industrial relations for Xerox Corporation West Coast operations, notes that "there's no graceful way to back down the ladder . . . unless you have a disability, taking a less stressful job is viewed as almost un-American."[40]

As with disparagement of racial or religious minorities, this negative view is, quite aside from the moral arguments, bad business. It wastes human potential and leads to time-consuming personal conflicts that can spill over into expensive litigation. In fiscal year 1985, 16,784 federal age-discrimination charges were filed with the Equal Employment Opportunity Commission, up 52 percent from 1982. Wrongful discharge was the leading category of claims, with 9,188 cases filed. Wrongful-discharge civil suits have also proliferated—most of them filed by middle-aged men fired for alleged poor performance.

Several companies have moved to avoid such outcomes in dealing with employees who are "burned out" by high stress or monotony or who cannot readily accept that their careers have indeed reached a plateau. Some examples follow.

Xerox has negotiated a voluntary downgrading option for unionized hourly workers in physically demanding or mentally stressful positions. Workers who are at least age 55 and have 15 years of service, as well as those age 50 and over who have 20 years of service, may bid on jobs at lower pay levels. Pay is set at the average between the former and the new job. Once an employee has exercised this option, he or she is ineligible for future promotions. Between 1980 and 1984, about 10 percent of the 450 employees eligible took advantage of the program. Although the downgrade program entails an effective wage-cost increase for Xerox, the company reports dividends in efficiency and lower absenteeism. Since pension calculations are based on an employee's best five earnings years, pension costs are not seriously affected.

IBM requires all managers to take at least 40 hours of training a year. In addition, professional and managerial employees participate in discussions relating to career goals and options. Some of these sessions are conducted by outside consultants such as Judith Bardwick, president of the management consulting firm In Transition, of La Jolla, California. She raises the "plateau" issue and suggests that it is a normal occurrence, not evidence of failure. She and others have found that when employees can accept this and overcome fear, anger, and frustration, they can direct their energies to previously neglected family relationships, avocations, and the possibility of a second career, while still giving a full measure of service to their employers.

Control Data Corporation has offered, since 1980, a mid-career course correction program to professional employees age 30 to 55. The three-day, computer-assisted course is based on the premise that employees sometimes need a career change and that it is better for them to explore options inside, rather than outside, the company. Control Data had found, for example, that a number of employees who had sought early retirement were seeking a career change. Under the mid-course correction program, employees sometimes transfer laterally to new career ladders. Retraining programs are in place to support this sort of mobility.

Future Trends

Forces in the social, political, legal, and technological environments will continue to require employers to look at and deal with older workers in new ways. However, experts disagree on the nature and direction of both the external changes and the appropriate corporate response.

As alternative employment strategies, programs for older workers are new only in the respect that they represent new thinking about the capabilities of these particular human resources. Operationally, they are but new applications of the profit orientation, imagination, and fundamental skills that are traditional hallmarks of good management. In developing such strategies, however, the employer community should heed a significant caveat:

> Today's older workers represent a specific generation whose experiences in this century do not match any future generation's. Their attitude toward work and their behavior in the workplace may be more a result of shared generational experiences than a result of maturity, and what researchers find to be true of older workers today may not be true ten, twenty, or thirty years from now.[41]

In Chapter 6, we will explore the implications of these differences in terms of a major shift from traditional employment relationships to contract employment.

Notes

1. E. Carlson, "Longer Work Life?" *Modern Maturity*, June–July 1985, 18.
2. K.W. Schair, quoted in B. Jacobson, *Young Programs for Older Workers* (New York: Van Nostrand Reinhold, 1980), 81.
3. Bureau of the Census, *True Level Population Projections* (1977), and Social Security Administration, *Social Security Area Population Projections* (1981).
4. President's Commission on Pension Policy, *Preliminary Findings of a Nationwide Survey on Retirement Income Issues* (May 1980). Appendix Item 5 to Special Committee, "Work After 65," part 2, 177.
5. S. Rich, "Majority of Firms Foster Early Retirement, Report Finds," *Washington Post*, 23 January 1985, F3.
6. M.H. Morrison, "The Aging of the U.S. Population: Human Resource Implications," *Monthly Labor Review*, May 1983, 13.
7. U.S. Congress, Senate Special Committee on Aging, *Personnel Practices for an Aging Work Force: Private-Sector Examples*, prepared for the Committee by L.S. Root and L.H. Zarrugh, 99th Cong., 1st Sess. (Washington, D.C.: Government Printing Office), 5–6.
8. For a comprehensive analysis, see B. Jacobson, *Young Programs for Older Workers* (New York: Van Nostrand Reinhold, 1980).
9. U.S. Congress, Senate Special Committee on Aging, *Work After 65: Options for the 80's: Hearing Before the Special Committee on Aging*, 96th Cong., 2d Sess., 13 May 1980 (Washington, D.C.: U.S. Government Printing Office), 102.
10. Ibid., 104–105.
11. Senate Special Committee on Aging, *Personnel Practices*, note 7, above, 41.
12. "Pink Slips for White Collars," *U.S. News & World Report*, 17 March 1986, 46.
13. Senate Special Committee, *Work After 65*, note 9, above, 111.
14. Ibid., 96.
15. R.P. Johnson and H.C. Riker, "Understanding the Capabilities of Mature Workers," *Four Modules in Small Business: Instructor's Guide* (Washington, D.C.: American Association of Community and Junior Colleges, 1982), 109.
16. N. Root, "Injuries Are Fewer Among Older Employees," *Monthly Labor Review*, March 1981, 30–34.
17. M. Doering, S. Rhodes, and M. Schuster, *The Aging Worker: Research and Recommendations* (Beverly Hills: Sage Publications, 1983), 77.
18. H.S. Parnes, ed., *Work and Retirement: A Longitudinal Study of Men* (Cambridge, Mass.: MIT Press, 1981), 158.
19. H.S. Parnes, et al., "From the Middle to the Later Years: Longitudinal Studies of the Pre- and Postretirement Experiences of Men," *Research on Aging*, December 1981, 387–402.
20. Yankelovich, Skelly and White, Inc., *Workers Over 50: Old Myths, New Realities* (Washington, D.C.: American Association of Retired Persons, 1985), 12.
21. Senate Special Committee, *Work After 65*, note 9, above, 107.
22. William M. Mercer-Meidinger, Inc., *Cost of Mandating Pension Accruals for Employees Aged 65–69* (Chicago: American Association of Retired People, 1985), 26.
23. Senate Special Committee, *Work After 65*, note 9, above, 108.

24. Senate Special Committee, *Personnel Practices*, note 7, above, 17.
25. Johnson and Riker, "Understanding," note 15, above, 107.
26. U.S. Department of Labor, *The Older American Workers: Age Discrimination in Employment* (Washington, D.C.: Government Printing Office, 1965).
27. U.S. Senate Committee on Human Resources, *Findings on Age, Capacity and Productivity* (Washington, D.C.: Government Printing Office, 1979).
28. Senate Special Committee, *Work After 65*, note 9, above 103.
29. E. Carlson, "The Plateau-Makers," *Dynamic Years*, March-April 1985, 33.
30. Jacobson, *Young Programs*, note 8, above, 74.
31. Johnson and Riker, "Understanding," note 15, above, 111.
32. Doering, et al., *The Aging Worker*, note 17, above, 113.
33. Johnson and Riker, "Understanding," note 15, above, 108, 109.
34. For a humorous and well-documented review, see H. Gittler, "One More Panacea and We'll All Go Nuts," *Industry Week*, 4 March 1985, 98–105, in which a seasoned engineer-executive traces his experience with four decades of management fads.
35. J.A. Byrne, "Business Fads: What's In—And Out," *Business Week*, 20 January 1986, 52–61.
36. S. Prokesch, " 'Intrapreneurship' Raising Doubts," *New York Times*, 28 July 1986, 19, 26.
37. Johnson and Riker, "Understanding," note 15, above, 111.
38. Senate Special Committee, *Work After 65*, note 9, above, 112.
39. Ibid., 95.
40. Carlson, "The Plateau-Makers," note 29, above, 34.
41. P.K. Robinson, "Research Update: The Older Worker," *Generations*, Summer 1982, 71.

5

Telecommuting

The term *telecommuting* was coined in 1973 by Jack Nilles, director of the Information Technology Program for the Futures Center at the University of Southern California at Los Angeles. However, the word has no widely accepted definition. This chapter will define telecommuting operationally as having the following characteristics that distinguish it from conventional work arrangements:

1. The work is performed at home by an employee for his or her employer, or at a satellite work center, or at a neighborhood work center. A satellite work center is a remote extension of the employer's office; it is located near the homes of a group of its telecommuters and is established primarily for their use. A neighborhood work center is a satellite center shared by several employers. The home or another telecommuting work center is the main work site for the employee, but telecommuters often attend meetings at the employer's offices. (In general, we will use the terms *employee* and *employer* to mean the telecommuter and the company engaging him or her, whether theirs is an employment or an independent contracting relationship. The distinction does have important legal implications, and will be addressed from that perspective elsewhere in this and other chapters.)
2. The work is of a type that would customarily be performed at the employer's office, to which—were they not telecommuters—employees normally must commute by car or public transportation.

3. Telecommuters may work full- or part-time, have fixed or flexible hours, have permanent or temporary status, and work a variety of shifts.
4. Not all telecommuters use regular or leased voice telephone lines and special equipment; some use normal or special mail delivery and regular telephone service to receive assignments, discuss problems, deliver their work product, and otherwise do business. According to Dr. Kathleen Christensen, Director, Project on Home-Based Work, City University of New York Graduate Center,

> Only one out of every four [home-based] clerical workers actually use some type of computer equipment in their work. The other three use typewriters, telephones, and pencils—the conventional tools of their trade. We can't help but conclude that for the majority, their cottages are electronic only to the extent they plug in their typewriters.[1]

Thus, while some observers associate telecommuting with telecommunications technology such as microcomputers, terminals, modems, telecommunications software, and the like, this chapter will include "telecommuters without computers" in its working definition. The key characteristics are the work site and the worker's relationship with a single employer. The telecommuter works at home, or at a special site near home, most of the time, as an alternative to commuting daily to the employer's office. To communicate with supervisors, subordinates, co-workers and customers, the telecommuter uses the mail and/or various forms of telecommunications. The communications may be the essence of the job, as with telemarketers, or incidental to it.

Telecommuters represent a wide range of clerical, technical, professional, and managerial occupations: examples are data entry, direct sales, computer programming, corporate accounting, design, analysis, research, law, and writing. Excluded from this definition are consultants, attorneys, accountants, typists, and other "homeworkers" who serve the public at large. According to Marcia Kelly, president of Electronic Services Unlimited Inc., a New York research and consulting firm, approximately 450 U.S. companies have telecommuting programs. These programs involve some 100,000 telecommuters. Nilles confirms this estimate and suggests that about 70,000 work at satellite centers and 30,000 at home. These figures exclude telecommuters employed by a number of state and local governments.

While there is much confusion about how many "teleworkers," "homeworkers," and the like there are, the figures just cited on telecommuting employees are consistent and probably reliable; they come from sources closest to the community of employers that have telecommuting programs. Among the prominent firms that have undertaken telecommuting programs are Shearson American Express, Chevron U.S.A., Inc., Control Data Corporation, Pacific Bell Telephone Company, Blue Cross-Blue Shield, J.C. Penney Company, and Apple Computer, Inc.

Telecommuting is in its infancy. Relatively few firms have tried it, and for those who have, very small numbers of employees are involved. But there is no question about the trend; employer interest in telecommuting is increasing steadily.

Case Histories

The case histories that follow show how corporations have taken advantage of the benefits of telecommuting, and how they have dealt (sometimes unsuccessfully) with the negative aspects. These firms represent different industries and regions, and their telecommuters perform different kinds of work. There is a pattern, however, in the factors that seem to add up to a successful telecommuting program, as well as in those whose presence may signal that telecommuting is ill-advised in a given company or work group.

Pacific Bell Telephone Company

Although it has employed telecommuters for only a year and a half, Pacific Bell no longer considers telecommuting a special program or project. "Now, it's just the way we work," says Rick Higgins, speaking for himself and some 90 other telecommuting managers at Pacific Bell. Higgins is telecommuting project manager for a Pacific Bell unit that studies and promotes telecommuting throughout the company and among the company's customers. He typically works two days a week at the company's satellite work center in Woodland Hills, California. The center is about a five-minute drive from his home, where he works the rest of the week.

Higgins reports to the company's corporate offices in San Francisco, but his clients are located in southern California. He works closely with study groups at the University of Southern California and elsewhere in southern California on telecommuting applications. By working from his home and from the Woodland Hills office, he can meet these responsibilities without relocating to San Francisco, as originally planned. Most of his associates at the satellite center report to Pacific Bell's offices in Los Angeles but deal with statewide issues or with client bases that are closer to their homes and to the satellite center. Marie Wax, for example, is a sales support manager responsible for one statewide corporate account. Telecommuting saves her three hours a day on the freeways and leaves her closer to her account's main office.

The managers using the Woodland Hills satellite center represent Pacific Bell's marketing, operations, and external affairs departments; they have subordinates as well as supervisors at the San Francisco and Los Angeles offices. In addition to Higgins, one manager uses the satellite center part-time, six use it full-time, and three use it on a "drop-in" basis.

The center was opened in June 1986 in an office building already leased by Pacific Bell at a cost of about $30,000. It provides partitioned offices and equipment such as personal computers, copiers, speaker phones, voice mail, facsimile equipment, file cabinets, and bookcases. It also has a 10-person conference room. The company opened a similar center near San Francisco in 1986.

Decision Factors

Several business reasons prompted Pacific Bell to investigate and adopt telecommuting. One reason was the need for increased competition in the telecommunications industry. Higgins explains,

> Consider an employee who works downtown and who has clients 25 or 30 miles away, where it takes an hour or so to get to them. If a customer calls at two in the afternoon and says, "Hey, can you come on out, we need you out here?" the employee may say, "How about tomorrow?"
>
> Well, if you tell them "How about tomorrow?" very often, they're going to be looking for somebody else. We're getting more competitive every day; you have to have people out where the clients are just to maintain your existing base.

Jim Campbell, a telecommuting Pacific Bell communications consultant, confirms Higgins' thesis. Before telecommuting, he faced a 26-mile freeway commute to his Los Angeles office. He would call on his customers early in the day or early in the evening, but avoided meetings at other times. Now he can meet his customers much more easily and thus is more productive.

Recruiting and retaining skilled employees continues to be a major factor. When it relocated 7,500 employees from its San Francisco headquarters to a new site 35 miles away in 1985, Pacific Bell permitted 15 computer maintenance people to telecommute from their homes, rather than risk losing them. Higgins notes that it can cost up to $40,000 to relocate an employee in California, and that training a new programmer can cost $110,000. The company also established a satellite office in San Diego for six fiber-optics specialists who did not want to participate in an office move. Linda Anapol, director of telecommuting, believes that without telecommuting these hard-to-find specialists would no longer be working for Pacific Bell. She also credits telecommuting with retaining one employee who would have resigned to have a baby and with returning three people from disability leave.

An office space shortage and high mainframe timesharing costs were other problems that Pacific Bell felt telecommuting might resolve, and the possibility of increased employee productivity was an additional factor in their decision. Other companies were confirming productivity gains of 15 to 20 percent from telecommuting, and it seemed intuitively obvious that by converting freeway time and tensions to productive energy, by working when they were personally most productive and relatively free of interruptions, employees would produce more and better work. Higgins puts it more bluntly: "If you get four hours [a day] worth of work out of an employee in a downtown office location, you're doing a fine job." As a telecommunications company, Pacific Bell had a special incentive to develop a model telecommuting program. To the extent that its customers follow the company's lead, they will buy more telecommunications equipment and services.

Initial Steps

Pacific Bell began by polling interested departments about the business problems they felt telecommuting might help resolve. Where such problems were identified and it was clear that the department, the manager, and the employee were interested, potential telecommuters were given questionnaires designed to gauge their suitability, and that of their jobs, for a trial program.

The no-nonsense focus on telecommuting as, first and foremost, a business tool, is evident from the first four items on the employee questionnaire:

1. What is the business problem to be addressed by the telecommuting arrangement?
2. How will you measure the success of telecommuting in terms of its providing a solution to that problem?

3. During what timeframe would you expect to realize the benefits of this solution?

4. What other benefits do you expect to realize and how can they be measured?

Other questions dealt with such issues as the employee's job duties and communications requirements (e.g., for face-to-face and telephone transactions) and his or her home situation in terms of having work space and a personal computer already in use. Although some of the candidates elected not to become telecommuters, none who became telecommuters has dropped out.

The company was equally cautious in selecting the "other half" of the telecommuting teams: supervisors of the telecommuters. Because of the minimal face-to-face communication involved in telecommuting, the supervisors had to be good communicators who were results-oriented rather than process-oriented.

Pacific Bell's philosophy is that for telecommuting to be successful management must define what the job is, including the employee's short- and long-range objectives. Company management studied the literature available on telecommuting, talked to other employers, and consulted with experts such as Nilles at the University of Southern California Center for Futures Research. They found that in most failed telecommuting programs management in effect said to some employees: "Here's a computer—go home and do it."

Higgins notes that in some telecommuting ventures that did not go well, employees were converted to outside contractor status. The company began to treat them as outside the mainstream, both socially and psychologically, setting up a self-fulfilling prophesy that led to conflicts. To avoid this situation, Pacific Bell decided to maintain its telecommuters on the same compensation and benefits programs, and offer them the same opportunities for advancement, as it does their counterparts at the office.

Trial Program

Various legal and employee-relations aspects of telecommuting were studied by Pacific Bell's legal and human resource staffs, and their views were incorporated into the trial program's design. The overall study of telecommuting possibilities was assigned to a six-member team that worked for more than a year before 45 employees were selected for a pilot program. Along with their supervisors, they received a half-day orientation program designed by the company which has since been refined and continued. The orientation covered some of the problems that new telecommuters often face, for example, guilt feelings, as well as friends, neighbors, and relatives who ask them to run errands and receive packages "since you're home all day anyway."

Pacific Bell has a written agreement with its telecommuters. Key elements include the following:

- A pledge that the employee's salary and employee benefits will not change as a result of the employee's participation in the program.
- Terms and conditions related to data security. Pacific Bell notes that such provisions are essentially "business as usual."
- Stipulation of a normal number of hours of work per week (40), with recognition that managerial employees may have to work in excess of 40 hours per week for the success or completion of a task (again, business as usual).
- A statement of the specific hours of work. This proviso is intended to prevent questions about workers' compensation should an employee be injured while working at home. Employees may change their hours (some do daily), but they are required to notify supervisors first so that the revised hours can be noted.
- A list of the furniture and equipment to be provided by the company.
- A clause reserving to the company the right to visit the home work site on 24-hours' notice. This is not a device for "checking up" on employees, but is motivated by safety concerns. For example, an employee may prefer to use personal furniture and equipment for a telecommuting work station. If the telecommuter's equipment is badly wired and a fire results, it is an open question as to whether the employer bears legal responsibility. Thus the inspection, and the underlying business necessity, are not that different from routine safety checks that companies make within their own walls.

The employees selected by Pacific Bell began telecommuting gradually. Even after their orientation program, they found they had to learn special skills as telecommuters. For example, frequent teleconferencing was required as a substitute for face-to-face meetings. As one manager explained,

> I would sit at my desk teleconferencing with a group of five people sitting in a room in northern California. The first few

times, they forget about you very quickly and start talking among themselves, and all of them start talking at once. We quickly learned to develop an advance, written agenda; one person in the room directed the comments of each participant on that end and kept bringing me back in for my response. He or she was the coordinator.

One telecommuter has the following method of dealing with the lack of verbal cues in teleconferencing:

You learn little tricks. For example, if I am talking to three colleagues, I'll put three chairs in my office with pictures of them. For a release, sometimes I'll throw something at them, a paper airplane or something. I'm not necessarily angry, but it breaks up the feeling of isolation and makes it more fun. But you still have to be a better listener because you still have more than one person talking sometimes, and you don't have any nonverbal cues. It has definitely improved my listening skills.

Home telecommuters and those using the satellite centers also coordinate by submitting advance schedules of the hours they intend to be available each week. Higgins, for example, heads a group of five other employees. From their weekly schedules, he makes up and distributes a matrix showing where each person plans to be at any given time during the week. Pacific Bell's telecommuters are encouraged to go in to their main offices at least once a week for face-to-face work updates and discussions with their supervisors, staffs, and co-workers. For many of them, it represents the only opportunity they have for face-to-face business and social interaction with their fellow employees.

In addition to communications problems, Pacific Bell had to overcome some work-related cultural barriers. Most employees are conditioned to believe that it is inappropriate to call co-workers and outside business contacts at their homes on day-to-day business matters. The company's early telecommuters found that this reluctance spilled over—inappropriately—to the telecommuting situation. One telecommuter found that in the middle of a conference call, someone would realize that he was at home and would ask, "Am I bothering you?"

Equipment needs were met in many cases simply by transporting office furniture, computers, and peripheral equipment from employees' offices to their homes and installing separate voice lines; in some cases, data transmission lines also had to be installed. At the satellite centers, telecommuters coordinate their schedules so that equipment can be shared. Due mainly to differences in file structure, there can be technical problems in setting up home work stations to handle transmissions between personal computers and central mainframe computers. Because many of the Pacific Bell telecommuters are technically trained, they have been able to overcome these problems. The company concedes, however, that less knowledgeable people would have a great deal more trouble.

Pacific Bell deliberately confined the trial program to managers to avoid the timekeeping requirements of the Fair Labor Standards Act and other regulatory burdens. "We wanted the maximum chance for success," Higgins says. And Pacific Bell does consider its telecommuting venture a success. Although 90 of the company's 70,000 employees are currently telecommuting, the company's careful screening and training approach has resulted in zero turnover among them. Several have been promoted.

The company is now analyzing the job content of such positions as systems analyst, programmer, budget analyst, and some categories of engineer for suitability for telecommuting. Because contract negotiations were under way when this book was in preparation, Pacific Bell would not comment on the possibility of negotiating at least a trial telecommuting arrangement involving union-represented employees. Other sources indicate, however, that it is a definite possibility.

Program Benefits

According to Pacific Bell's management, telecommuting has achieved net cost reduction goals in each of the targeted categories. Floor space costs have been reduced. The company prefers not to give specific figures, but it is possible to make a rough estimate. If one assumes an annual floor space cost of $6,000 attributed to one office worker, converting the better part of 90 employees to home telecommuting and the others to combined home and satellite center work (space costs at satellite centers may be half the cost of space in nearby major cities), the savings are obvious. Pacific Bell has also saved on mainframe timesharing costs; their telecommuters can send and receive data at off-peak hours.

There is an additional benefit in reduced turnover. By eliminating the grueling daily rush-hour commute for the highly skilled management and professional employees who make up its telecommuters, Pacific Bell has no doubt that it has prevented defections. When the earlier-cited costs of recruiting, relocating, and training are considered, retaining just one professional through telecommuting "will buy a lot of computer equipment," says Higgins.

Although traditionally hard to measure in management positions, the productivity of Pacific Bell's telecommuters may represent the greatest cost savings realized by the telecommuting initiative. Managers and employees tend to agree that greatest productivity occurs when employees perceive that their work goals are in harmony with personal needs and goals. Academicians call it "congruence." The testimonials by Pacific Bell's (and other firms') telecommuters are interesting in this regard; they tend to shift their frame of reference between the personal benefits telecommuting has brought them and their ability to work more productively and creatively as managers. The following comment by a Pacific Bell employee is typical:

> The opportunity to telecommute . . . allows me about 15 to 20 extra hours per week to devote to my family or my projects. It not only helps the gas bill, but allows me to work in a very productive atmosphere without unnecessary interferences.

J.C. Penney Company

In Milwaukee, the main commuter problem is not freeway gridlock, as in southern California, but "iceblock." The snowy weather in Milwaukee posed a special problem for the J.C. Penny Telephone Sales Center, where sales associates take catalog orders. Unexpected peaks in telephone orders required the center's manager, Carl Kirpatrick, to try to reach associates at home during their off hours and ask them to come in to work. Often, by the time a willing employee was reached, got dressed, perhaps made hurried arrangements for child care, then drove to the center, the peak demand had passed and potential sales had been lost. And although the associate would be paid for her time, she was not likely to be enthusiastic about having her home life disrupted and making the trek, possibly through a snowstorm, essentially for nothing. Kirpatrick and his sales associates no longer have that problem. In 1981 the company began a telecommuting experiment that became a highly successful program.

Twenty J.C. Penney associates now work at terminals in their homes in Atlanta, Columbus, Ohio, and Milwaukee. They respond to customer calls routed to them by automatic call distributors from 14 telephone sales centers, which employ 8,000 to 9,000 part-time associates throughout the country. The sales associates average 15 to 20 hours per week, but may be required to work 30 to 35 hours per week during peak periods.

While Penney's telecommuters thus differ from those at Pacific Bell in important respects, that is, they are part-time, nonmanagement employees, the two companies are remarkably similar in their management philosophy and approach to telecommuting as a staffing strategy. The telecommuting associates at J.C. Penney receive the same pay, employee benefits, and opportunity for advancement as their counterparts who work at the centers. In one case, the telecommuting experience produced a "backspin"; an experienced associate turned down a promotion that would have required her to return to the center.

Employee Selection

As at Pacific Bell and other companies with successful telecommuting programs, employees were selected carefully. Kirpatrick first surveyed 165 associates, of whom 120 were willing to try telecommuting. Seven were selected for the first trial. The company first looked to employees experienced in all phases of order-taking and customer assistance who had demonstrated their ability to work under pressure during peak periods. (Penney's does 50 percent of its catalog business in a period of about six weeks.) Candidates for telecommuting were further screened for their ability to work relatively independently.

Program Benefits

Inclement weather was not the only reason for adopting telecommuting at J.C. Penney. The company reports savings in construction and office space costs. It plans to expand the program if necessary, rather than build new sales centers or expand existing ones. With regard to employees' on-the-job productivity, Kirpatrick comments that telecommuters have more of a feeling of being one-on-one with the customer, and thus a higher level of responsibility. Their relative productivity is generally better than that of the office-bound associates. Penney's conclusions about productivity are based on more than anecdote, however. Management has access to daily reports from the Call Director System verifying the number of calls handled by each associate and the average time required per call.

Supervision

J.C. Penney has found that the key to successful supervision of telecommuters is "better planning and consistency." One observer who is familiar with a number of telecommuting programs put it less delicately: "Let's face it. You can get away with a lot in sloppy management when your people are sitting right outside your office; you can race out and tie up a lot of loose ends." Indeed, most of us have seen the supervisor who appears to be doing "a heck of a job" but is, in fact, frenetically—and frequently—backing and filling to correct the results of poor planning, coordination, and communication (although the problem may originate at higher levels than that of the supervisor).

To help bring about a more consistent approach, the J.C. Penney program

- Uses electronic and regular mail to handle administrative procedures such as those related to time sheets, work schedules, personnel notices, paychecks, and catalog changes.
- Features a broadcast screen that transmits messages to the associates' home terminals. If, for example, a supervisor would like an operator to call the office, that message can be transmitted on-line.
- Provides for face-to-face meetings every two to three months so that problems and procedures can be discussed. Supervisors also visit the telecommuters at their homes, after making advance arrangements, and encourage them to visit the center to keep in touch with co-workers.

So far, there has been no turnover among the J.C. Penney telecommuters, and peak-load scheduling problems are virtually nonexistent. When unexpected high volumes occur, Kirpatrick is able to contact an off-duty telecommuter at home and request her to log on, rather than ask her to drive to the center, as before. The company plans to expand the program and has a long waiting list of office-bound associates, representing all 14 centers, who would prefer to work from home.

Equipment and Costs

The hardware used by Penney's telecommuters is the same as that used in the centers. Two telephone lines are required—a

voice line for the customer's call and one for subsequent transmission of the order data from the telecommuter to the center's
mainframe computer. Kirpatrick points to one potential cost problem. J.C. Penney has experienced a substantial increase in the cost
of running off-premises extension (OPX) lines to its telecommuters'
homes. The company is trying to get around the problem by developing technology and having equipment built to its own specifications.

Best Western International, Inc.

While Californians contend with gridlock, and Milwaukeeians
with iceblock, Best Western's telecommuters work from cellblocks.
In 1981, Best Western established a satellite reservations center
inside the Arizona Center for Women (ACW), a minimum-security
correctional facility. This venture now employs 30 inmates as reser-
vation sales agents. They handle reservations requests during peak
times through a toll-free reservations number. The reservations
center operates from 5:00 A.M. to midnight, or as dictated by call
volume. Best Western originally equipped the center with 20 CRT
stations and the necessary telephone lines, and in 1986 the facility
was expanded to 30 stations. Best Western began the program to
answer the same business need as J.C. Penney—to have a flexible
work force that could report to work within minutes to handle call
overflow.

In its first five years, the center generated more than $72
million in room bookings, and it now handles 10 percent of the
company's U.S. call volume. Potential agents at ACW are first
screened by the Department of Corrections. Applicants must not
have a record of fraud, and they must be able to type 20 words
per minute, be sales-oriented, and have a good sense of geography.
ACW reservations agents are paid the same salary as other Best
Western agents, starting at $4.42 per hour with an increase of up
to 12 percent in six months if performance is satisfactory.

In addition to helping Best Western solve its staffing problem,
the program benefits the state, the community, and the inmates.
The ACW reservationists pay federal income and FICA taxes on
their earnings, and 30 percent of their net earnings are deducted
for room and board. A percentage of the balance may be sent home
to help support their families; the remainder is held in reserve
until their release. "We are getting something back as taxpayers,"
notes Wendy Black, corporate communications director. "The ACW

reservations agents learn a marketable skill, and many have made enough money to take their families off welfare."

The Best Western-ACW program has been acclaimed by former U.S. Supreme Court Chief Justice Warren Burger. However, Best Western was driven primarily by the same profit motive as are other companies with successful telecommuting programs. The firm's chief executive officer, Ron Evans, explains,

> We were aware, of course, that it would be beneficial to the community, but that wasn't our primary consideration. It [the telecommuting program] has been successful in part because it is self-serving. A partnership can only be successful if it works for all partners. . . . And we have the ultimate commitment to the program; we hire many of the women when they're released.[2]

Since its inception, more than 152 inmates have worked for Best Western at ACW and 34 of them have been hired by Best Western upon release. Currently, 16 ex-ACW reservations agents work at Best Western headquarters in Phoenix, Arizona. Of those, nine have been promoted to clerical positions in marketing, membership administration, and reservations. Best Western has found the productivity of the ACW agents at least equal to that of their other agents. The inmates are eligible for the same incentive bonuses and frequently win them. Other firms, such as TWA, have had similar positive experiences with inmate telecommuters.

Cal-Western Insurance Company

Not all telecommuting programs have fared as well as those just discussed. In 1983, a subsidiary of American General Insurance Co., Cal-Western Insurance Co. of Sacramento, California, offered its experienced medical insurance claims processors the opportunity to work at home as telecommuters. They would process claims via terminals connected to the company's mainframe computer. If they accepted, however, they would be required to resign as employees and sign an independent contractor agreement. The agreement set weekly production quotas and gave Cal-Western the right to immediately terminate the agreement if a telecommuter failed to make quota. The agreement also stipulated that the "contractor" would hold the company harmless and indemnify it if the company were sued for improper claims processing. The agreement also required the contractor to advise Cal-Western if he or she processed claims for any other insurance company, so that Cal-Western could terminate the agreement if it so chose. The home processors would lease their computer terminals from Cal-Western for $50 per month.

Legal Issues

Intrigued with the prospect of eliminating the daily commute to work and having greater flexibility in and control over both their work and their family lives, 22 of the employees—all women—agreed. As of 1985, eight of the women, who had had from 3 to 11 years of service with Cal-Western before the telecommuting arrangement, had terminated their agreements and sued the company in California Superior Court in Sacramento for approximately $200,000 in back benefits, including recovery of Social Security taxes they were required to pay as "independent contractors." They sought an additional $1 million in punitive damages. The key legal issue in the Cal-Western case is whether or nor these were true independent contractors or de facto employees of Cal-Western.

While it is not necessarily binding on the court that will hear the lawsuit, the plaintiffs' attorney, Roderick MacKenzie, notes that when the women applied for state unemployment compensation, "The [state agency] looked at the contract the women had with the company and literally laughed at it; they proclaimed them all employees and granted them unemployment compensation."[3]

When a House subcommittee invited American General Life Insurance Co., parent company of Cal-Western, to testify at a public hearing on home-based clerical work, the company sent a letter declining to testify on the grounds that to do so would be "inappropriate."[4] Standing uncontroverted, the plaintiffs' story appears a strong indictment of the company's motives and business practices.

Basically, the plaintiffs claim that (1) Cal-Western increased the original work quota, requiring the women to work from 12 to 15 hours a day to meet it; (2) the company's computer system frequently failed, forcing the telecommuters to work according to the computer's erratic schedule; and (3) the company continuously dictated to them the procedures and methods by which they were to process the claims, and frequently changed those methods and procedures.

For obvious reasons, the Cal-Western case is being watched closely. Many observers with a stake in telecommuting fear that Cal-Western may prove the lawyer's adage that "hard cases make bad law" and that it will prompt Congress to "fix" abuses simply by banning all home work arrangements, as the AFL-CIO has recommended. It is perhaps ironic that neither MacKenzie nor his clients suggest such a throw-the-baby-out-with-the-bathwater approach. The *New York Times* reports that despite their experience with the program, the Cal-Western telecommuters would consider working at home in the future. "I would be willing to accept another job at home, if it were done properly," said one of the women.[5]

Telecommuting's Role in the Management Process

Telecommuting, like all alternative employment strategies, is a management tool. As the case histories cited in this chapter suggest, it has been used most effectively where applied to focused business goals such as lower costs and higher productivity. As management weighs this new tool, direct and indirect costs and benefits must be defined and measurement standards agreed to. Whether done formally or informally, consideration should be given to long- versus short-run payback, internal rates of return, and other factors that go into any investment that could be costly on the front end and disruptive should it fail. And as in any such analysis, companies will differ as to the proper variables and their relative weights in the analysis. But the analysis must be made to ensure the best decision.

The best decision may be not to attempt telecommuting; the experts are unanimous that telecommuting is not wise for all companies and operations. Gil Gordon, president of Gil Gordon Associates, a Monmouth Junction, New Jersey, consulting firm, comments that he worries when he sees a company start telecommuting "for experimentation, when there is no clear business benefit in sight." He and others are concerned that there may be a number of telecommuting failures if companies adopt this option simply because others are doing it.

Advantages of Telecommuting

When it has been carefully thought out and used to contribute to specific business goals, telecommuting has brought significant benefits to companies of all sizes in the following areas.

Lower Floor Space Costs

As Lehrer has pointed out in *White Collar Productivity*,

In the traditional office the great bulk of cost was incurred for labor. Increasingly, however, costs are now being incurred for data-processing equipment, specialized office automation, special materials, supplies, and even air conditioning, all of which have become important in the overall calculation. It is certainly wise to make a quick review of the importance of nonlabor costs before assuming away the need to analyze other than partial labor productivity. If these nonlabor costs are important, they should be explicitly recognized in whatever measurement system is developed.[6]

Floor space certainly represents one significant, nonlabor cost for management to consider. According to consultant Gordon, businesses that rent office space pay anywhere from $2,000 to $6,000 per employee per year. Other experts say that floor space costs as high as $12,000 per year per employee are not uncommon in some urban areas. Employers can get a rough idea of what space costs can be by multiplying the going rate per square foot for office space rental (or construction and maintenance) by these typical allocations:

Employee Category	Square Feet Required
General office worker	65–80
Supervisor	100–120
Secretary	150
Administrative executive	300

(If corridors are adjacent, 50 to 100 square feet should be added per office.)[7]

Directly or indirectly (when leasing), management must also bear the expense of acquiring and maintaining nonproductive space such as cafeterias and vending areas, mail rooms, rest rooms, building maintenance and equipment rooms, and parking lots. Insurance and property taxes are additional, often substantial, overhead expenses.

When considering new or expanded facilities, management has traditionally considered these expenses as unavoidable; the only question has been: In what manner shall we bear them, that is, do we build or rent? Telecommuting presents a new option by asking:

Why do either, if existing facilities, already insured, maintained, and essentially tax- and overhead-free can be adapted at nominal cost? Those "facilities" are, of course, employees' homes.

Gordon suggests another dimension to the work-space factor: Reducing space through telecommuting can be seen as more than reducing a "dead overhead cost," he says. It can, in some cases, increase revenues. He recommends that companies explore telecommuting possibilities when planning construction of new office buildings. They could then "overbuild" to the extent of providing footage for full staffing, and rent to outside tenants any unneeded footage made available as a result of telework arrangements. Gordon says that some employers located in prime office space areas are already eyeing their existing space as possible profit centers. These companies are considering assigning some employees to telecommuting and subletting their former offices to other tenants at premium rates. For a company already short of space, telecommuting can help prevent overcrowding people, which adversely affects productivity. Converting office space from an expense to a revenue account would, of course, require a strong commitment to telecommuting by both management and employees; a decision to rent out existing space cannot be readily reversed once staff members convert to telework and their offices are given over to outside parties.

Lower Recruiting Costs

Telecommuting allows an employer to cast a wider net, to recruit people who cannot or will not come in to the office on a regular 9:00-to-5:00, five-day-a-week schedule. This becomes especially important when there is a high demand for people with scarce talents. As Gordon puts it, "It isn't so much the technology driving it as it is the fact that those people are in short supply. Some of the companies using telecommuting find that it is one of the few ways they can attract good people."

Lower Turnover Costs

Telecommuting has also been found to aid in retaining good employees. The cost savings from reduced turnover can be substantial. According to a survey of 400 firms conducted by Costello, Erdlen & Co., a recruiting firm based in Wellesley, Massachusetts, it costs, on average, $8,580 to hire an experienced new employee, and, when hiring a large number of technical personnel, the average cost per hire exceeds $10,000.[8] Gordon cites a case that occurred while he was on the human resources staff of Johnson and Johnson. The firm had a biostatistician who left the company because she had a young child with serious health problems. She and the company tried juggling her work schedule, but it did not work out.

> She had been hired at a salary of $22,000 per year, and when she left, she was at $28,000; she was doing exceptionally well—a top performer.
> We replaced her with someone who was relatively an unknown quantity at a starting salary of $30,000, and paid an employment agency fee of $8,000. The woman who left us went out and started doing consulting, working out of her home. We never should have lost that person.

Higher Productivity

In terms of both quality and quantity of work output, telecommuters appear to be more productive than their office-bound counterparts. Most companies with successful programs report productivity gains of 10 to 40 percent. In some cases, those improvements can be quantified. With respect to the J.C. Penney sales associates, for example, the systems that direct customer calls to both the telecommuters and their counterparts at the sales centers track the number of calls handled by each associate and the average length per call.

Telecommuting can also increase labor productivity by providing more flexible schedules for the operation of mainframe computers. Today, office employees who interact with mainframe computers from desk-top terminals or personal computers can spend a lot of time tapping their fingers while waiting in the "queue." This is because companies typically try to compress 80 to 90 percent of the demand on the mainframe into daytime business hours. This forces them into a Hobson's choice between poor labor productivity and expensive investment in additional mainframe capacity. Telecommuting offers an alternative by allowing companies to spread the workload over two or even three shifts. This is essentially what telephone companies have been doing for years in offering lower long-distance calling rates at off-peak hours.

Improved Business Climate

It does not appear that any of the successful telecommuting programs were established for reasons of "corporate citizenship," "social responsibility," or "good public relations." Yet they have enhanced their sponsors' public images in several ways. A number of people with physical disabilities are productively employed only because telecommuting allows them to work at home. Other telecommuters are prison inmates. Receiving the same pay as their counterparts at the employer's office, these inmates pay income taxes; and, in some programs, part of their earnings is returned to the state or federal government to offset the cost of their incarceration, and to provide restitution for their crimes. Because these programs present such an unusual "win-win" outcome, they have attracted good publicity for participating companies. Telecommuting also can contribute to a more civic-minded community simply by allowing employees to spend more time in their neighborhoods. Pacific Bell's Higgins comments,

> Politically, we're so apathetic. But if I'm in the community, driving over roads with potholes five days a week, or using mass transit, trying to get around to the shopping centers, and not just going downtown every day [to the office], I'm going to start asking who's running things in my home town. I'll notice things I never noticed before because I'm not on the freeway all day. And by putting men back in the community again we can get involved in things like Boy Scouts and Little League.
>
> When a company establishes a satellite office in the suburbs, people no longer think of it as "that big outfit downtown." You have established a corporate presence in that neighborhood. All this comes back to benefit the corporation in the long run.

Disadvantages of Telecommuting

There are several drawbacks to telecommuting as a human resources management strategy, including those that follow.

Service Charges

As a result of the AT&T breakup, local telephone companies are expected to raise rates to business customers. According to Frederick G. Withington, vice-president for information systems at Arthur D. Little, Inc., local rate regulators will necessarily extract the maximum possible revenues from high-cost local business services to subsidize consumer telephone service, and to make up for the local long-distance subsidy. Thus, even though a leased line has the same technology and the same potential for price decline as the long distance one, it will in fact increase sharply in cost.[9]

Withington and other experts point out, however, that there are ways around local telephone service such as private microwave links, unregulated leased lines, cable television, and other media. Management should identify and carefully evaluate these factors before subscribing to communications services whose costs are controlled by the supplier.

Legal Concerns

Telecommuting can lead employers into some murky legal areas. Most employment-related laws and regulations assume that employees commute daily to their employer's place of business, work eight or so continuous hours, then return home. State and federal laws are unclear with respect to such issues as workers' compensation liability, maintenance of safety standards, and affirmative action requirements as they relate to telecommuters.

Ronald J. James, an attorney with the Cleveland-based law firm of Squire, Sanders & Dempsey, notes that it is much more difficult to organize people who are telecommuting via computer from many locations than it is to organize those same people when they are sitting in one room in a downtown location. "So the unions are clearly going to be against these developments," he observes. The AFL-CIO is now pressing for a total ban on telecommuting.[10]

Incompatibility With Management Style

Telecommuting is not compatible with every organization's management philosophy, nor with the management styles of some individual supervisors. Hewlett-Packard Company, for example, tried telecommuting at its Colorado Springs Division, but no longer encourages the practice because, says personnel manager John Caldron, "We're better served by people being here."[11] Likewise, telecommuting will be resisted—and if implemented will almost surely fail—where supervisors lack the planning and communications skills and the basic personal beliefs essential for true management by objectives.

Firms that have tried telecommuting, individual supervisors, consultants, academicians, and others are unanimous in their conclusion that telecommuting makes a good supervisor better and a poor one worse. They also agree that this holds true for employees as well; if a person is a problem office worker, making that person a telecommuter simply gives management a problem telecommuter—and one over whom it has even less control.

Possible Rejection by Employees

Even where telecommuting may be compatible with a company's management approach, it clearly is not compatible with the needs and expectations of every employee. Employees who need a great deal of personal interaction on the job and those who need fairly constant direction and feedback from their supervisors (including nonverbal communication), will not be successful telecommuters. One computer programmer who first warmed to the idea of working at home returned to working at the office. He missed the interaction with people, and since the working hours were not well publicized, people called him at any hour.

Irreversibility of the Telecommuting Decision

A decision to implement telecommuting may be difficult to alter. In many cases, a telecommuting venture gone awry cannot be corrected simply by returning employees to the office. A number of employees may have been moved out of a central office to work in their homes or at a satellite center. The work space left behind may be leased to outside tenants or devoted to other uses. In other cases, some level of telecommuting may be assumed in space planning for a new office, and management may not have a place to put the displaced telecommuters if telecommuting does not work out.

Future Trends

Estimates of the future number of telecommuters vary. In part, this is because predictions vary as to the strength of management resistance to the attitude changes sometimes required for successful new telecommuting ventures. There are also varying assumptions about labor-market and other forces that could either hinder or spur the telecommuting trend. Most such inconsistencies can be traced to the definition problems encountered in trying to get at current numbers. The high predictions—of upwards to 20 million "teleworkers" by 1990—usually include "cottage-industry" proprietors and even people who use their own personal computers to catch up on paperwork brought home from the office.

Whatever the rate, however, telecommuting will probably continue to grow, and with an increasing success rate, for four reasons. The first reason is demographic; the work force will continue to be better-educated, more computer-literate, and more self-directed. Second, we will continue to become more and more a nation of information workers and service providers—dealing in the kind of input, processing, and output that lends itself well to telecommuting with or without computers. Third, telecommunications technology is becoming increasingly more manageable for nonspecialists, applicable to a greater range of tasks, and less expensive. Finally, as companies study the experiences of other firms, learning from both successes and failures, they will be more confident in moving ahead, where a telecommuting venture seems indicated.

If telecommuting receives a major setback, it will most likely be in the form of restrictive legislation responding to labor's warnings about "electronic sweatshops" and "exploitation" of home workers.

Within any individual company, however, the basic attitudes of top management may be the greatest obstacle for the human resource professional or line manager interested in telecommuting as a staffing strategy. According to one consultant,

> I've talked to many companies that understand the economics, but their managers just aren't ready to try something new. We have a population of managers who are used to supervising by observing activities rather than by measuring performance or results.
>
> Managers have also been brainwashed to believe that bigger is better. Look at the job evaluation systems that award points for bigger staffs, budgets, and span of control. Under that system, managers' negative reactions to telecommuting are understandable.
>
> You have to provide a carrot. Top management could, for example, offer to return to executives' bonus pools a certain percentage of the value of floor space saved through telecommuting.
>
> You are utilizing gain-sharing; you need to link the benefits of telecommuting to rewards that make sense to the managers involved. If they see it only as a taking away of part of their

empires, and an affront to tradition, why should they support it?

Such advice is worth heeding, but we must recognize that managers will bite on the carrot only if they have both the skills and the attitudes necessary to try telecommuting and make it work. One observer noted, "Telework does not call for more trust; it calls for careful assessment and reapplication of the trust that is necessary for organizational performance in the first place."[12]

To the extent that a company's current supervisory and management styles, its approach to job design and personnel policies, and the attitudes of its employees show that such trust is fundamentally lacking, management is not likely to embrace telecommuting. It is just as well. Pacific Bell's Higgins notes that at some other companies where he has presented the telecommuting concept, managers have responded that they would be wary of telecommuting because they do not trust their employees.

> When you hear that, you know you've got a big problem up front. If you have a company that is mismanaged, that is disorganized at all, that has employees that you might not be able to trust, you'll rip it apart with telecommuting. But if you take a company that is on the way with goal orientation, that is well-organized, you're just going to enhance that with telecommuting; you're going to make a better manager and a better employee.

It is likely, then, that there will be a continuing process of natural selection. Many believe that firms whose human resource management approach is based on trust, openness, good communications, and interest in results rather than procedures, will, in the main, be the survivors in today's and tomorrow's competitive environment. If that is so, telecommuting will continue to help many such firms ensure that survival.

Managers with the "overseer" view of human resource management will understand quite well what Higgins is saying. It is a sad irony that their rejection of the very thought of telecommuting will prove one of their wiser management decisions. How long such companies will be around to reflect on that wisdom is another question.

Notes

1. U.S. Congress, House Subcommittee on Housing and Employment, *Pros and Cons of Home-Based Clerical Work: Hearing Before a Subcommittee of the Committee on Government Operations*, 99th Cong., 2d sess., 1986, 22–23.

2. From a Best Western brochure, "A Good Way to Do Bad Time."
3. "Telecommuters Sue Employer, Claiming Improper Use of Independent Contractor Status," *Telecommuting Review: The Gordon Report*, 1 February 1986, 11.
4. House Subcommittee, *Pros and Cons*, note 1, above, 106.
5. A. Pollack, "Home-Based Work Stirs Suit," *New York Times*, 26 May 1986, Y18.
6. R.N. Lehrer, *White Collar Productivity* (New York: McGraw-Hill, 1983), 32.
7. D.F. Roberts, *Marketing and Leasing of Office Space* (Chicago: Institute of Real Estate Management of the National Association of Realtors, 1979), 138.
8. "Paying for Job Candidates," Labor Letter Column, *National Business Employment Weekly*, 8 December 1985, 1.
9. C. Sandler, "Communications," *Personal Computing*, October 1986, 95.
10. See D. Chamot, "Ban Work at Home; It Exploits Workers," *USA Today*, 28 March 1986, 8A.
11. J. Friendly, "Change With Computers: The House Becomes an Office," *New York Times*, 15 May 1986, Y17–19.
12. T. Miller, "Telecommuting Benefits Business with DP's Help," *Computerworld*, 17 February 1986, 4.

6

Individual Employment Contracts

Traditional Approaches to Employment Contracts

Written contracts between individuals and their employers
have existed for many years. Annual contracts are traditional among
nontenured faculty in higher education, and more open-ended
agreements are common among top corporate executives. Such
arrangements cover only a small percentage of the work force,
however; the vast majority of managers and unrepresented rank-
and-file workers have no written agreement setting forth the terms,
conditions, and duration of their employment. Their relationship
is governed by the common-law doctrine of employment at will:
that an employment relationship not of fixed duration may be terminated at the will of either party. Because of the individual nature
of personal employment contracts, there are no hard data available
on the number of them in existence.

Current Trend Toward Individual Contracts

Despite the lack of specific data, there are signs that the use
of individual contracts is growing as an alternative strategy for
employer and employee alike. David M. Richardson, president of
Richardson & Rundel, a management recruiting firm in Upper
Montclair, New Jersey, finds that increasing numbers of middle
managers who change jobs insist on employment contracts or detailed letters of agreement. He notes too, that higher-level managers who once relied on letters of agreement are insisting on formal

contracts. "I think now formal contracts are used for most jobs paying $75,000; compared with three years ago when $100,000 to $125,000 were the salary ranges usually commanding employment contracts." Another executive recruiter, David E. Chambers, chairman of David Chambers Associates Inc., New York, has observed that the trend began to intensify in 1982, with managers at the $50,000 level requiring specific details in their letters of agreement.[1] Allan Kennedy, co-author of *Corporate Cultures: The Rites and Rituals of Corporate Life*, indicates that many professionals now work under employment contracts, and he believes that they will become uniform.[2]

Employment Contract Provisions

In addition to the normal offer-letter provisions such as starting salary and date, employment contracts or letters of agreement for middle managers typically contain the following:

- A statement that the employment relationship is "at will" and may be terminated by either party for any reason.
- Provision for severance pay in the event the employee is terminated. Severance may be linked to a notice period; for example, the employer may terminate the employee with two weeks' notice and five weeks of severance pay, or with no notice and five weeks of severance pay. Other provisions may be made for such things as outplacement assistance and forgiveness of relocation loans in the event of termination.
- A requirement that, as a condition of receiving accrued vacation pay or other such benefits, the employee give some minimum notice of resignation.
- A statement as to the frequency of and procedure for performance appraisals and salary reviews.
- Incorporation by reference of employee handbooks, benefits literature, work rules, and other agreements such as confidentiality pledges with respect to the company's proprietary information.
- A statement that the agreement constitutes the entire agreement between the parties and can only be modified in writing. Of the specific provisions of an employment contract, this one may be of potentially greatest value to the employer. It provides some safeguard to the employer from

the effect of "recruiting puffery" or oral assurances of tenure made in the hiring process.

- For higher-level executives, the contract may also cover incentive compensation, stock option grants, and "golden parachute" provisos as appropriate.

An employer that maintains a policy of *generally* terminating employees only for cause, and after progressive disciplinary action or some form of internal due process, is not precluded from firing a worker summarily, and without establishing cause, if it retains the right to do so in the employment contract. There is nothing inherently wrong with using words such as "usually," "in most cases," or other qualifiers in either the employment contract or the employer's written termination and discipline policy. The key is that the relationship between the two documents be clear and that the employer both says what it means and means what it says.

Advantages of Individual Employment Contracts

There are several reasons for the increasing popularity of personal employment contracts.

Avoiding Misunderstandings

A formal employment contract offers the same advantages as any other. It makes relatively clear the rights, responsibilities, and intentions of both parties and serves as evidence that they have agreed on them. It thereby protects each party from the adverse consequences of misunderstandings that can arise from oral and implied contracts. Since the mid-1970s, for example, the Motorola Semiconductor Product Sector has hired production assemblers under individual contracts. (There is no union at the semiconductor facilities.) In 1974 and 1975, a downturn in the semiconductor business required the company to lay off 8,000 of some 18,000 workers at its Phoenix, Arizona, and Austin, Texas, plants and close down the latter facility. When the industry rebounded, the company began hiring production workers on six-month, renewable contracts. Over time, the contracts evolved into 12-month agreements for ease of administration.

The contracts provide the new workers the same employee benefits eligibility and working conditions as other employees, with the following exceptions:

- The contract employees are not guaranteed reinstatement upon return from medical leave.
- The contract employees have one less step in their grievance procedure than regular employees.
- The contract provides that either party can cancel it upon 24 hours' notice.
- Contract employees are ineligible for severance pay.

The Semiconductor Sector tries to maintain roughly 15 percent of its direct labor force in contract status. When production staff must be pared, their contracts are cancelled before regular employees are let go. Upon recall, the previous service accrued by the contract employees is recognized. Assuming satisfactory performance, these workers may be converted to regular employee status at the end of the contract term, with credit for past service. In addition to providing a buffer to protect regular employees from layoff, the contract arrangement allows Motorola ample opportunity to evaluate new personnel before deciding to make them regular employees. The vast majority of them ultimately convert to regular status.

In substance, the Motorola arrangement is not much different from conventional employment arrangements. Employees are hired with a probationary period (one year is longer than most) during which time they have fewer entitlements than regular workers and they understand that they will be laid off before regular workers and may be dismissed somewhat more arbitrarily. All these provisions could be, and at other companies are, handled in a personnel policy manual. A Motorola spokesman explains: "The only real difference is that you go into the hiring situation with an absolute agreement that says 'you guys are cannon fodder—if war comes, you will be the first to go.' It's an up-front agreement that either you or [we] can give 24 hours' notice, and it's goodbye."

Minimizing Legal Liability

Given the demise of the psychological contract and the related constructs of trust and loyalty, it is clear why today's employees are inclined to say, "Put it in writing." Allan Kennedy explains that people will no longer enter into situations in which they can be fired arbitrarily if they and their employers "don't hit it off."[3] And, because of the crumbling of the employment-at-will doctrine, employers are being persuaded that it is in their interest as well to have the employment relationship spelled out. Attorney Ronald James notes,

> With this whole new wave of jury awards and erosion of employment-at-will, I've been telling our clients that if they don't make their own contracts, then some third party, a judge or a jury, is going to make a contract for them. At the middle-management to executive, white-collar level—and even the high-skilled technician level—it's an excellent idea for management to provide written employment contracts.

The "Bottom Line" in Performance Appraisal

Most managers agree that, except where an employee is clearly deficient in job performance, the traditional performance appraisal is an empty ritual. It is usually a one-way communication by which a supervisor tells a subordinate directly or indirectly how big a salary increase to expect. Concepts such as "promotability" and "development" may be discussed and noted, but often in vague terms. In some cases, the supervisor has "inherited" a subordinate whose job performance is marginal. Most managers are reluctant to terminate such a person because they do not wish to "rock the boat" or risk legal actions, or because it would violate their own or the organization's sense of fairness. This is especially true when the employee has been with the company for a long time.

The employment contract of fixed duration, however, allows—indeed, *requires*—management to ask periodically, "Would we hire this person today?" and to act on that evaluation. The approach of the annual contract review should similarly prompt the employee to ask: "Would I accept a job offer from this company today?" If either party is dissatisfied with some aspect of the relationship, the contract review process provides a framework for frank discussion and negotiation.

Foundation for a Reality-Based Relationship

As implied in the comments of the Motorola official quoted earlier, the greatest advantage of the written contract for both employee and employer is psychological. It presents the employment relationship for what it is: a business arrangement of uncertain duration between a seller and a buyer of services—both seeking to maximize their own benefits. It is a welcome antidote to any lingering traces of the cruelly absurd notion of the corporation as "family," with its concomitant promise of lifelong personal commitment, caring, and stability.

The personal employment contract is not a panacea for poor communications and evaluation techniques, nor does it allow employers to side-step legal concerns. For example, in its decisions as to whose contract is renewed and whose is not, management is bound by the same nondiscrimination rules regarding selection standards and their application as it is with respect to any personnel decision. There will be employees and supervisors who see no substantive difference between "We've decided not to renew your contract" and "You're fired." However, by basing the employment relationship on a straightforward acknowledgment of the realities of business life, the employment contract paves the way for an association that in most cases will be more productive, more candid, and less stressful to all parties than one based on vague, unfulfillable promises and unrealistic expectations.

Disadvantages of Individual Employment Contracts

Administration

Just as formal employment agreements offer the same advantages as other contracts, they also have the same potential disadvantages. For example, they require administration and, in some cases, negotiation. As noted by author Kennedy and the management recruiters cited earlier, managers and executives who are sought for job openings are bringing their own contracts to the table. These contracts are often prepared by lawyers. When the employer takes the initiative as to contract terms or makes counterproposals, the executive may review the employer's recommendations with an attorney. Such deliberations take time.

Except at top executive levels, where special compensation programs are often negotiated, the contract issues important to today's manager usually center on the "down side" of the relationship. These include notice of termination, severance pay, pension and savings plan withdrawals, and outplacement and relocation assistance. Many of the executives in the current job market have gained their knowledge of such affairs by hard experience. In many cases, the potential new employer has in place reasonable policies on these subjects that can be set out in the contract or be incorporated by reference. Some executives are able to negotiate considerations beyond the standard policy, avoiding the expensive litigation that can result years later if such prehire accommodations are promised orally.

Once agreed to, the individual employment contract must be drafted and maintained. If it is of fixed duration, subject to renewal, a system must be developed to allow for review, discussion, and if necessary, timely notice of intent to terminate. Administration of contracts is complicated in organizations that transfer management employees among operations, but no more than it is with respect to performance appraisal systems.

Problems With Retroactivity

If management decides to hire new employees under individual contracts, what does it communicate to current workers? Few companies will wish to suddenly confront a stable work force of long-term employees with the news that management reserves the right to fire them at will. If management does not do so, however, while hiring new staff under such a stipulation, is it effectively granting tenure to current employees? There appears to be no significant case law on this question, but it is an issue for management and counsel to consider in weighing the implications of contract employment relationships.

Potential Problems With Nonmanagement Employees

The existence of an employment contract does not necessarily insulate an employer from successful legal actions by terminated employees. Some employers may argue that since employees have the same right as employers to terminate employment contracts, they should receive no special consideration from the courts. The California Supreme Court has noted, however, that "when viewed in the context of present-day economic reality and the joint, reasonable expectations of employers and their employees, the 'freedom' bestowed by the rule of law on the employee may indeed be fictional."[4] Attorney James points out that, especially at lower job levels where applicants are more vulnerable and less sophisticated than sought-after executives, a contract may not be upheld if it lacks the basic standards of fairness and due process that the courts and juries are applying in unjust-dismissal cases.

Union Organizing Concerns

Some observers suggest that contracts that remind unrepresented workers of their vulnerability to arbitrary dismissal play into the hands of union organizers. However, union attacks on the lack of worker protection in individual employment contracts are not difficult to counter by a management that has a sound employee relations program. Motorola has had no serious organizing threats in the 15 years it has been using individual employment contracts. The factors that influence workers in representation elections go well beyond any one issue. If employment contracts for new workers signal the start of a successful organizing drive in a particular company, that company is due to be organized and probably deserves to be.

Future Trends Toward Individual Employment Agreements

Like other forms of alternative employment strategies, the use of individual, written employment contracts will, in all likelihood, become more common because they benefit both employer and employee. Events of recent years have largely destroyed the concept of "a career with X Corporation," as Jeffrey J. Hallett, president of Trend Response and Analysis Company, Alexandria, Virginia, correctly notes:

> The likelihood of working for the same organization for more than 10 years is very low. The reason for this is that the likelihood of any company having a clear idea of what it will be doing in 10 years is low.
> For those working as full-time, dedicated, career-oriented employees for large organizations, what was once a well-defined career path is now an anxiety-laden jungle . . . everyone in every job knows that "job security" is a contradiction in terms.[5]

Presented with the opportunity to work for another company, prudent individuals will no longer view it with rose-colored glasses, but from the standpoint of what *Business Week* has termed "Me, Inc."[6] They will view it as an arm's-length and, in all likelihood, temporary association.

Management, too, has learned the negative consequences of work force dislocation. It is not anxious to expose itself to the disruption, lawsuits, and bad publicity stemming from employees' sense of betrayal. As long as these quite compatible perspectives reflect the reality of the workplace, straightforward, written contracts spelling out the limitations of the employment relationship will serve the interests of employer and employee alike.

Notes

1. E.M. Fowler, "Managers Insisting on Contracts," *New York Times*, 17 October 1984, D25.
2. "Agent Recruiters," *National Business Employment Weekly*, 17 November 1985, 10.
3. Ibid.
4. *Cleary v. American Airlines, Inc.*, 111 Cal. App. 3d 311, 171 Cal. Rptr. 917 (1981).
5. J.J. Hallett, "Redefining Retirement," *Personnel Administrator*, November 1986, 26, 28.
6. B. Nussbaum, et al., "The End of Corporate Loyalty," *Business Week*, 4 August 1986, 44.

7

Common Concerns About Alternative Employment Strategies

Employers typically express concerns about the alternative employment strategies outlined in this book. These concerns tend to fall into three categories: legal/regulatory issues, quality control, and attitudes of regular employees and supervisors toward workers hired under nontraditional arrangements.

Legal and Regulatory Issues

A full legal analysis is beyond the scope of this book. What follows is a discussion of some of the broad issues often raised by legal experts with respect to alternative employment strategies.

Common-Law Rules Governing Independent Contractor Status

For a company weighing the legal ramifications of an alternative staffing arrangement, the first question to resolve is whether or not those who would perform services under the arrangement would be independent contractors, employees of a third party such as a THS firm, employees of the recipient of their services, or employees of both the recipient and the third party. If the employer's counsel determines that the workers would be or could be held to be employees of the company, or that a joint employer relationship would exist, the company may wish to go no further. Alternatively, it might modify the arrangement under consideration to avoid such an outcome.

An advantage of considering the employment status issue first is that, if employment status is correctly defined, the employer's legal obligations and risks become relatively clear. As noted in Chapter 5, the legal criteria for determining the employment status of workers do not rest on what an employer calls the workers. Just as an employer may not declare certain employees exempt from the Fair Labor Standards Act simply by calling them "managers," it may not confer true independent contractor status on them merely by so designating them. The courts, taxing authorities, state workers' compensation boards, and administrative agencies that enforce employee protection statutes rely on various common-law tests to determine whether an individual (or a group of workers) is in fact an employee or an independent contractor. Under the Internal Revenue Code, for instance, the key factual issue is the extent of control the employer has over the worker and over the manner in which the work is performed. The Code states,

> Generally, the relationship of employer and employee exists when the person for whom services are performed has the right to control and direct the individual who performs the services, not only as to the result to be accomplished by the work but also as to the details and means by which that result is accomplished.[1]

Michael L. Solomon, an attorney for Hahn, Loeser, Freedheim, Dean & Wellman, of Cleveland, Ohio, indicates that under IRS rules "it is not necessary that the employer actually direct or control the manner in which the services are performed; it is sufficient if he has the right to do so. The right to discharge a worker is an indication of the employer/employee relationship."[2] Other factors that the courts and administrative agencies review include the duration of the relationship between the worker and the recipient of his services and the extent to which the worker performs services for other employers.

The Joint Employer Doctrine

In certain cases, courts and administrative agencies will determine that two employers exercise control over a worker or group of workers, and that they are thus joint employers. These determinations are sometimes made by the National Labor Relations

Board in determining organizing rights of employees seeking union representation and in resolving secondary boycott issues. The Board and the courts will determine joint employer status between two or more employers when they "share or co-determine those matters governing essential terms and conditions of employment." The factors looked to in these cases include hiring and firing; promotions and demotions; setting wages, work hours, and other terms of employment; discipline; and day-to-day supervision and direction of the employee.[3] Client companies often play an active role in these matters under employee leasing agreements and, to a lesser extent, in selecting and directing THS firm employees assigned to them.

Essentially the same test is applied in discrimination cases. In a federal sex discrimination suit, the plaintiff, a lobby attendant, was employed by a company that performed cleaning services under contract with a building management company. A district court found that the building management company had trained the attendant, established her job duties, and supervised her day-to-day work. The building management company also distributed instruction manuals to lobby attendants and to other ground-floor personnel. The court concluded that the cleaning contractor and building management company were joint employers and could both be held liable for discrimination.[4]

As suggested in Chapter 3, employers considering contract staffing should carefully define the degree of control they wish to exercise in personnel decisions, and they should review the legal implications of those expectations. There is nothing inherently unwise about a joint employer relationship; the point is that both employers must recognize and define it at the start.

Statutory Rules Governing Independent Contractor Status

The Tax Reform Act of 1987 (Section 1706) has tightened the standards for determining, for tax purposes, whether a technical service worker assigned to work for a company through a third party such as a job shop is in fact an independent contractor or an employee. Technical service workers include engineers, designers, drafters, computer programmers, systems analysts, and those engaged in similar work. Each case that comes under IRS scrutiny will be viewed on its own merits; however, the IRS will apply the "generally applicable common law standards," and it is expected that if the company obtaining a technical service worker's services substantially controls the work performed, *if the individual runs no risk of losing money on a project*, or if the person performing the services works on the premises of the company, it may be unlikely that this person can receive the tax benefits of an independent contractor. (Emphasis added.)[5]

If the IRS determines that technical service workers hired through a third party are in fact employees of the recipient, the employer may be penalized for failure to withhold income and Social Security tax and may be liable for retroactive pension- and other benefit-plan funding to which the individual is entitled as an employee. In such circumstances, the recipient may also be responsible for workers' compensation coverage.

Government Security Requirements

The revised Department of Defense (DOD) Industrial Security Manual effectively eliminates the authority of defense contractors to issue low-level security clearances to THS firm temporaries assigned to their facilities. Prior to the revision, DOD had delegated authority to THS firms to issue "company confidential" clearances to such workers. The new procedures require the THS firm to clear its employees through the DOD Defense Investigation Service. According to the National Association of Temporary Services, the time required may adversely affect customer service.[6] For the employer with government contracts involving classified data or facilities, these procedures are an additional factor to consider in deciding whether, or how extensively, to use THS and job-shop personnel.

State and Federal Safety and Health Statutes

When employees such as the Pacific Bell and J.C. Penney telecommuters work in their homes, what are the employer's responsibilities under state and federal laws that set safety and health standards for the workplace? In addition to setting specific standards in such areas as air quality, noise levels, and machine guarding, for example, the federal Occupational Safety and Health Act (OSHA) imposes on the employer a "general duty" to provide employees with a workplace that is "free from recognized hazards that are causing or are likely to cause death or serious physical harm to his employees."[7] According to legal experts, an employer may raise lack of control over a hazard as a defense to an alleged violation, but may also be required to show that it took reasonable measures to protect its workers. As an example, a home telecommuter might use adapters to connect work lighting, a personal computer, printer, and other peripherals to a single wall outlet. Although there appears to have been no significant case law in this area to date, an employer might be held responsible for an injury caused to the employee as a result of an electrical hazard posed by such wiring. It may thus be advisable for employers of telecommuters, as well as other home workers, to visit their homes routinely to inspect work stations for possible hazards.

Equal Employment Opportunity Requirements

Even where workers are clearly the employees of a third party such as a THS firm, government contractors covered by Federal Executive Order 11246 are subject to a "pass down" requirement. Under that requirement, the contractor's subcontractors must certify that they have affirmative action plans and unsegregated facilities, and that they otherwise meet the obligations of both EO 11246 and Title VII of the Civil Rights Act of 1984. Attorney James notes that a subcontractor may be subject to more stringent requirements than a prime contractor, but that it is the prime contractor (e.g., a company using THS temps) that is responsible to its government contracting agency and to the Office of Federal Contract Compliance for the compliance of the THS firm. The federal contractor that engages in extensive use of THS temps to "avoid EEO hassles" may thus be in for a rude surprise. If it wishes to avoid such a surprise, it may find it more difficult to monitor the hiring practices of temporary help suppliers than to monitor its own.

Quality Control

Of 328 employers responding to a BNA survey, 45 percent listed "quality control problems" as a factor limiting their use of flexible staffing. It should be noted that the concern is expressed not in terms of the quality of the work as such, but, properly, in terms of management's ability to *control* that quality. Part of this concern can be explained by the fact that the survey included in its definition of "flexible staffing" the contracting-out of entire operations. In such cases, as with contract maintenance, for instance, control of the work is completely in the hands of the contractor's own supervisory staff; in some such cases, the work may be done off the client's premises. It is clear from the case histories and other examples given that companies that *are* pleased with the quality of work performed under alternative staffing strategies have carefully thought through and implemented the quality control measures required.

Such measures have included, for example, the assessment of both employee preferences and supervisory skills in selecting telecommuters at Pacific Bell; the ad hoc and periodic review of THS firm performance at Johnson and Johnson Products; and the standardized job and skill requirement descriptions used by Manpower Temporary Services, Inc., in matching workers to specific client needs. In addressing the quality control issue, then, management must determine the following:

- What constitutes quality job performance.
- What the specific measurement criteria are for such performance.
- How (and whether) the criteria could be timely applied under an alternative staffing arrangement.
- How management would make the adjustments necessary to improve individual performance where it may fall short.

In some cases, management will find that it can exercise more effective control over work output by employing regular staff. In other cases, it might adopt a combination strategy such as Bank of America's simultaneous use of THS temps and those from its own temp pool.

Workplace Attitudes

As noted in Chapter 1, the increasing prevalence of a "contingent work force"—upon which alternative employment strategies are centered—reflects many changes in technology, individual and family life-styles, and personal and corporate priorities. As with other social and economic shifts that affect such basic institutions as family and workplace, these developments are sometimes resisted. To the extent that alternative employment strategies represent such changes, they will be discouraged by some managers and regular staff.

At several points, this book has highlighted the similarity between workplace resistance to specific alternative employment strategies and resistance to inclusion of women and minorities in nontraditional jobs. The analogy holds with respect to alternative employment strategies in general. For example, resistance to the concept of the career woman was a combination of truly held beliefs that women lacked the inherent temperament necessary for success, that they lacked true commitment to work, that they would take jobs from "real breadwinners," and that they would otherwise damage the institution of the family. Just as such stereotypes reinforced resistance to changing roles for women in the workplace, similar stereotypes reinforce opposition to alternative employment strategies: Older workers can't keep up, therefore they should make way for younger workers; temporary employees have a "short-timer" attitude; telecommuters just want to stay home, and so forth. Moreover, just as placement of ill-prepared blacks and women in unreceptive environments produced failures that seemed to justify negative stereotypes, management now sets up self-fulfilling prophesies about the decline of the older worker's abilities and motivation.

In cases of outright misuse of alternative strategies, the suspicion and hostility of regular staff are appropriate. At the Maryland research and development facilities of one large corporation, for example, approximately 20 clerical and secretarial employees were given six weeks' notice of termination in connection with a corporate "downsizing." These employees were told that they would be replaced by THS temporaries until management could determine the exact organization structure required by the lower staffing levels. To qualify for severance pay, the employees were required to spend the last two weeks of employment training their replacements. Nine months later, the THS employees were still there. Vacancies in permanent positions unaffected by the staff reduction now are filled by agency temps who are screened, interviewed, and selected by company management for "indefinite assignment." Regular employees who have seen their friends fired speak bitterly of the "permanent temps," and they are reportedly seeking union representation. Several of the temporary workers have asked for reassignment because of hostility from the survivors of the staff reductions.

There are other potential abuses of alternative staffing arrangements. In an article in *Personnel Administrator*, one personnel director outlined, among others, the following "advantages" to having an in-house temporary help service:

- It can be used as a way to circumvent "no-relative policies" and employ relatives of current employees.
- It can be a way to hire and "hide" qualified employees for whom no full-time position exists.[8]

In other cases, management may simply fail to communicate convincingly the purpose of alternative work arrangements. Despite a positive employee relations climate and nationally noted success with other alternative staffing approaches, one company cited in this book abandoned a plan under which retirees performed plant maintenance at night on special "minishifts." Although it was not management's intent, regular workers saw the program as a step toward replacement of permanent staff with part-time workers.

Alternative employment strategies often require supervisors with better-than-average planning and communications skills. To the extent that supervisors lack such skills, their resistance to new ways of working is a natural response. In such cases, management must decide whether it is more effective to try to upgrade those skills or to assume the far more difficult task of altering supervisors' leadership styles to facilitate successful new employment strategies.

Clearly, then, concerns about bringing in workers under nontraditional arrangements are, in some cases, valid, and alternative staffing will prove unsuccessful for some organizations. The key question for top management is whether such concerns are valid in that they represent a thoughtful analysis of decision variables, or whether they are potential agents of a self-fulfilling prophesy based on unfounded fears and misconceptions. As the case studies in this book have shown, organizations can both realize benefits and avoid costly mistakes when top management discards preconceived ideas, focuses on specific goals, and applies basic management decision-making principles to its analysis of alternative employment strategies.

Notes

1. Regulations of the Internal Revenue Code of 1954 as amended, Sec. 31.3401(c)-1, 31.3121(d)-1, and 31.3306(i).
2. M.J. Solomon, from a monologue published for a seminar, "Staff Leasing: A Staff Management and Tax Advantage Tool," sponsored by Hausser & Taylor, Hahn, Loeser, Freedheim, Dean & Wellman, and National Employer, Inc. (Cleveland, Ohio: May 1986), 9.
3. J.V. Jansonius, "Use and Misuse of Employee Leasing," *Labor Law Journal*, 1 January 1985, 36.
4. Ibid., citing *EEOC v. Sage Realty*, 507 F. Supp. 599, 24 FEP 1521 (S.D.N.Y., 1981).

5. L. Sloane, "Self-Employed and Tax Law," *New York Times*, 24 January 1987, 34.
6. National Association of Temporary Services, *Legislative Outlook*, 22 December 1986, 5.
7. 29 U.S.C. Sec. 654(a)(1).
8. G.T. Huddleston, Jr., "One Way to Reduce Temporary Help Costs," *Personnel Administrator*, January 1985, 10.

Appendix A

national technical
services association

NTSA RECOMMENDED PRACTICE

HOW A CLIENT SHOULD PURCHASE
CONTRACT TECHNICAL SERVICES

NTSA DOCUMENT 674 • RECOMMENDED PRACTICE JULY 1974 EDITION
© 1974 NATIONAL TECHNICAL SERVICES ASSOCIATION
1255 Twenty-Third Street, N.W. • Washington, D.C. 20037 • (202) 452-8100

Reprinted by permission of the National Technical Services Association.

FOREWORD

Contract technical services are intangible commodities and, therefore, it is very difficult to compare the services proposed by several different suppliers. The National Technical Services Association, which is the only major organization representing all of the contract technical service industry, has prepared this brochure to assist the clients of its member firms to purchase contract technical services more efficiently and effectively. One of the main functions of this brochure is to increase appreciably the quality of communication between the client and prospective supplier. In providing intangible services, communication breakdowns sometimes occur between the client and the supplier, resulting in disappointments to either or both parties, and possibly even causing the discontinuance of the service contract.

Experience has proven that if a complete and detailed understanding exists between the client and the supplier as to responsibilities, authorities, and other considerations, there is substantial opportunity for a richly rewarding and successful business relationship. It is the intent of this brochure to do all that is possible to establish and to insure this excellent business relationship.

In the preparation of this brochure, many clients and suppliers have been contacted for the benefit of their experiences, and this article therefore represents an authoritative cross-section of the best thinking on the subject. If clients apply the principles set forth in this brochure, they too will experience good results in the use of contract technical services.

PROCEDURES

When a client recognizes a need for contract technical services, there are a number of questions that must be considered in order to procure most efficiently the best services available. These questions involve such matters as: size, complexity, scope, and duration of the work to be performed; urgency of the program; and its importance in the client's overall scheme of business.

If the project is of critical importance to the client's operation, or is large, vast in its scope, or long in duration, then the client should use sophisticated procurement methods, such as the two-step procedure described later in the brochure.

If the project is of a low order of criticality, of moderate scope and complexity, and of relatively small size, then a single-step procedure, or even informal negotiation with known suppliers, would be a satisfactory method of procurement. If the particular program has a critical time schedule, there may be sufficient time to complete only a single-step procurement or informal negotiation.

Many clients have found that if a small requirement of modest duration exists, informal negotiation, such as a telephone call with a known supplier without the attendant expenses of a formal quotation, is the most efficient manner to handle that procurement.

Annual Basic Agreements

Many clients have found that if they have continuing needs of a fluctuating nature throughout the year, their most efficient procedure is a two-step procurement establishing basic agreements with several suppliers, wherein the suppliers agree to provide the specified services for a one-year period at predetermined conditions and billing rates. Then the clients merely order the services from this basic agreement as their needs dictate.

Single-Step Procurement

A single-step procurement is defined as one in which the client sends out formal requests for complete proposals to a pre-qualified list of suppliers. The responses received must be comprehensive in every respect, including price, description of how the service would be performed, and all other data comprising a complete proposal. The client then makes his contract awards on just that information.

Two-Step Procurement

A two-step procurement is one in which the client sends out two separate requests for proposals: First, the business/technical qualifying proposals (excluding pricing data) and, secondly, to those who qualify, the cost proposals.

These requests can be sent out either to a pre-qualified list, or to anyone wishing to respond to the request.

The business/technical proposal defines the supplier's technical capability, management of the program, and all other data describing the supplier's solution to client problems together with the reasons the supplier feels most qualified to complete the program. The client then reviews and evaluates these business proposals, selects three, five, eight or more of the most qualified suppliers, and then requests their submission of a cost proposal. The client then evaluates the dual proposals, and awards either a sole source or multiple contract for the program.

Number of Suppliers

A decision that the client must also make relates to the use of one or several suppliers. At first, one might think that this decision would be based solely upon a client's ability to find a supplier who can provide all of the client's needs; however, many other factors need be considered.

Many clients have found that they obtain substantial benefits from the award of multiple contracts in that the results of the competition between two suppliers to out-perform each other greatly out-weigh the additional administrative burdens resulting from working with more than one contractor. Sometimes a client will pick a small supplier and a large supplier, or may award as many as five or more contracts to different suppliers.

Some clients have found it advantageous to award multiple contracts on large volume or highly complex projects. However, there are always the isolated instances wherein the nature of the project or the manner in which it needs to be performed, precludes using more than one supplier.

To obtain effective utilization of more than one supplier, it is of utmost importance that each supplier be given equal opportunity to obtain his fair share of the client's business. It is incumbent upon the client to set up strict administrative procedures so that each supplier is notified simultaneously of any new requirements or changes in scope on the project.

Small or Large Suppliers

Some clients find advantages in working with a small organization whereby the day-to-day contact is with a principal of the supplier. By working with such a principal, it may become much easier for a client to receive full attention from the supplier on any problem that may arise in the relationship between them. There are other instances where a client will find that a small supplier may be much more capable of providing specialized service than a large supplier, because of the specialized experience that the smaller supplier possesses.

FORMAL REQUEST FOR PROPOSAL

It is very important that all suppliers get the same information in preparing their quotations.

An important element in the two-way communication between the client and the supplier is the formal Request For Proposal. Listed below are suggested items that the client should include in his Request For Proposal so that the supplier will have all of the information necessary to properly prepare his response.

Also included is a list of items that we suggest the client utilize in evaluating the supplier's response. It may be that the client would want to "weight" or group some of these items so that their greater importance to the client will be emphasized. It would be a relatively easy matter for the client to set up a numerical evaluation system whereby a total point count can be obtained on each potential supplier.

Information Defined by Client

It is recommended that at least the following information be defined in order to communicate adequately to potential suppliers the estimated size, scope, and duration of the project:

a) Detailed description of the work to be performed and/or a detailed description of the education and experience required of the personnel needed.

b) Definition of where the work is to be performed.

c) Specification of workweek in anticipated hours/day and hours/week.

d) Definition of initial manpower schedule, including the start date for each classification of employee required, and/or work to be performed.

e) Definition of anticipated manpower increases or decreases for each classification, with expected dates of such changes.

f) Definition of anticipated termination date of each classification of employee required, and/or work to be performed.

g) Specification of security classification of work.

h) Definition of technical responsibility of contract technical service company.

i) Definition of administrative responsibility of contract technical service company.

j) Definition of method of approval and acceptance by client of employees.

k) Definition of termination notice period that client will give upon termination of any given employee (excluding notice for cause or incompetency).

l) Definition of basis for pricing, such as cost per hour (S.T. and O.T.), cost per unit of work, or cost per project.

m) Definition of minimum insurance coverages required.

n) If per diem living expenses are applicable, definition of client policy on reimbursement to contract technical service company for employee's per diem living expenses.

o) Definition of client policy on reimbursement to contract technical service company for employee's transportation costs at beginning and end of program.

p) Definition of the facilities, materials, supplies, and equipment to be furnished by client.

q) Definition of the facilities, materials, supplies, and equipment to be furnished by the contract technical service company.

r) Identification of specific holidays and plant closings that client celebrates or experiences.

s) Identification of specific holidays that client expects contract technical service company to pay its employees.

t) Specification of time and date the proposal is to be submitted.

u) Specification of expected date of award of contract.

v) Specification of number of contracts to be awarded.

w) Definition of items that will be considered in determining winning contractor(s).

Client Evaluation of Response to Request for Proposal

To insure a thorough evaluation of suppliers' full capabilities, listed below are a number of items that are felt to be most pertinent for clients to consider in judging responses from those suppliers:

a) Technical capability of supplier.

b) Depth of management of supplier.

c) Price (total price/unit of work or/hour).

d) Resumes of people proposed for the job who have specifically agreed to accept the job; and/or
Resumes of people currently on supplier's staff who fit the qualifications requested by the client.

e) Size of supplier in number of current employees and annual volume.

f) Financial strength of supplier.

g) Credit position of supplier.

h) NTSA membership of supplier; and/or
Willingness of supplier to guarantee his adherence to the NTSA Code of Ethics (Attached).

i) Quality of supplier's proposal.

j) Quality and capability of supplier's management staff.

k) References of current clients utilizing similar type services; and/or
References of current clients utilizing any of supplier's services.

l) Extent of supplier's work for past or present clients for similar work indicating dollar volume, date, and client reference.

m) Degree of responsiveness of supplier to client's Request For Proposal.

BID CONFERENCE

There may be occasions where the scope of the program is so complex or difficult to define in writing, that a bid conference is appropriate. Unfortunately, many times bid conferences are a one-way communication from client to potential supplier because the potential suppliers are many times reluctant to ask questions which may either show their lack of understanding of the project, or may bring out knowledge which may benefit their competitors.

PRE—AWARD CONFERENCE

If the project is complex or broad in scope, it may be beneficial for the client to have individual conferences with the potential winner(s) of contracts, so that the client can explore in greater depth the capability of each supplier to handle his portion of the client's project.

11/85-950

Appendix B

STANDARD FORM OF AGREEMENT

for

TECHNICAL SERVICES

on

**TIME AND MATERIAL BASIS ON
SERVICE COMPANY'S PREMISES**

AGREEMENT

BETWEEN

_____

AND

_____

RECOMMENDED BY THE NATIONAL TECHNICAL SERVICES ASSOCIATION

NTSA DOCUMENT 771 • MEMBER-CLIENT AGREEMENT (COMPANY'S PREMISES) JULY 1971 EDITION
©1971 NATIONAL TECHNICAL SERVICES ASSOCIATION • 1255 Twenty-Third Street, N.W. • Washington, D.C. 20037 • (202) 452-8100

Reprinted by permission of the National Technical Services Association.

**NTSA RECOMMENDED
STANDARD FORM OF AGREEMENT**

**For Technical Services
On Time And Material Basis On Service Company's Premises**

TABLE OF CONTENTS

2

NTSA DOCUMENT 771 • MEMBER-CLIENT AGREEMENT (COMPANY'S PREMISES) JULY 1971 EDITION
© 1971 NATIONAL TECHNICAL SERVICES ASSOCIATION • 1255 Twenty-Third Street, N.W. • Washington, D.C. 20037 • (202) 452-8100

AGREEMENT

THIS AGREEMENT, made this_____ day of _____19_____ by and between

_____ (hereinafter called CLIENT)

and _____ (hereinafter called COMPANY).

WITNESSETH:

That, whereas the CLIENT desires technical services to be performed *on the COMPANY's premises* by employees of the COMPANY, and whereas the COMPANY agrees to provide such employees to perform such technical services.

NOW, THEREFORE, the CLIENT and the COMPANY in consideration of the mutual covenants hereinafter set forth and intending to be legally bound hereby AGREE as follows:

ARTICLE 1

COMPANY EMPLOYEES

1.1 Independent Contractor –

COMPANY is an independent contractor. The personnel assigned to perform work for CLIENT on COMPANY's premises are employees of COMPANY and are hereinafter called EMPLOYEE or EMPLOYEES. Such EMPLOYEES shall be paid for their services only by COMPANY. All matters concerning wages, expenses, hours worked and paid, working conditions, and other similar administrative matters shall be resolved between EMPLOYEE and COMPANY and not between EMPLOYEE and CLIENT.

1.2 Satisfactory Performance –

If any EMPLOYEE assigned to CLIENT's work does not satisfactorily perform his assigned duties, or if CLIENT considers EMPLOYEE's conduct detrimental to CLIENT's overall program, COMPANY shall withdraw such EMPLOYEE immediately upon CLIENT's notification. CLIENT shall be responsible to pay COMPANY for the period of time EMPLOYEE was assigned to CLIENT's work.

1.3 Solicitation of Employees –

Neither CLIENT nor COMPANY shall solicit, approach or hire any of the other's employees for the purpose of employment by the other so long as this agreement is in effect and shall not have been terminated and for a period of ninety (90) days thereafter, except with the written consent of the other party.

1.4 Equal Employment Opportunity –

COMPANY and CLIENT agree to apply uniform and equitable standards of employment opportunity and assure that the best possible use is made of the abilities of EMPLOYEES regardless of race, creed, color, sex or age.

1.5 Employee Section –

EMPLOYEES shall be selected by COMPANY in accordance with COMPANY's understanding of CLIENT's technical requirements, and all work performed by these EMPLOYEES shall be billable to CLIENT under paragraph 3.2 until CLIENT notifies COMPANY in accordance with paragraph 1.2 above.

—— 3

NTSA DOCUMENT 771 • MEMBER-CLIENT AGREEMENT (COMPANY'S PREMISES) JULY 1971 EDITION
© 1971 NATIONAL TECHNICAL SERVICES ASSOCIATION • 1255 Twenty-Third Street, N.W. • Washington, D.C. 20037 • (202) 452-8100

ARTICLE 2

PROPRIETARY INFORMATION – INVENTIONS AND DISCOVERIES

2.1 Proprietary Information –

COMPANY informs its employees that private or proprietary information of its clients may become available to them. COMPANY instructs its employees to maintain such confidentiality and, where requested, requires that employees agree in writing substantially as follows:

2.2.1 *All information (pertaining to COMPANY's or its clients' inventions, designs, tools, equipment, unpublished written materials, plans, processes, costs, methods, systems, improvements, or other private or proprietary matters) which is obtained by employees in the performance of their work and which is not publicly disclosed by COMPANY or its clients shall be considered as private and proprietary to COMPANY or to its clients whoever supplies or provides such information. Employees shall not, at any time during or after such employment, disclose such information nor the nature of the service which they render for COMPANY or its clients, except to authorized representatives of COMPANY or its clients.*

The foregoing provisions in this paragraph shall be for the benefit of both COMPANY and its clients to whose work COMPANY's employees are assigned, and either COMPANY or its clients shall have all rights and remedies to enforce such provisions.

2.1.2 COMPANY will assign to clients, where requested, all of COMPANY's rights and remedies under the above provisions.

2.2 Inventions and Discoveries –

COMPANY requires each of its employees to execute an agreement which assigns to COMPANY, or its nominee, all and any discoveries and/or inventions as specified in paragraph 2.2.1 below. COMPANY will assign to clients, as its nominee, COMPANY's rights under these agreements.

2.2.1 The agreement states in part as follows:

All and any discoveries and/or inventions (which shall include improvements and modifications, but shall not be limited thereto) relating to work performed by employees, or relating to matters disclosed to employees in connection with work to be performed, or suggested by such matters, whether or not patentable, which discoveries and/or inventions are made or conceived by employees, solely or jointly with others, during the term of their employment (regardless of whether conceived or developed during working hours), or during a period of one (1) year thereafter, shall be the property of COMPANY or its nominee and such discoveries and/or inventions shall be promptly disclosed to COMPANY.

COMPANY, or its nominee, shall have the right to file and prosecute, at its own expense, all patent applications; whether U.S. or foreign, on said discoveries and/or inventions. Employees shall, during their employment, at any time or times thereafter, provide to COMPANY or its nominee, all documents, information and assistance requested for the filing or prosecution of any such patent application, for the preparation, prosecution or defense of any legal action or application pertaining to such discoveries and/or inventions and for the assignment or conveyance to COMPANY, or its nominee, of all right, title and interest in and to such discoveries and/or inventions, patent applications and letters patent issuing thereon. Employees shall, in addition to the foregoing, upon request by COMPANY, execute and deliver to COMPANY such agreements, pertaining to discoveries and/or inventions, as may at any time during the period of employees' employment, be requested of COMPANY by clients, to whose work employee is assigned.

ARTICLE 3

RECORDS

3.1 Accounting Records –

COMPANY shall maintain complete and accurate accounting records in accordance with standard accounting practice to substantiate all charges hereunder. Such records may include payroll records, job cards, attendance records and summaries, and COMPANY shall retain such records for a period of three (3) years from date of final invoice.

3.2 Time Records –

COMPANY will provide each EMPLOYEE with weekly time tickets and/or time cards. Such time records shall be maintained by EMPLOYEE on a daily basis and, at the end of each week, the hours of work of each EMPLOYEE assigned to CLIENT's work shall be approved by CLIENT. These CLIENT approved time records will be used by the COMPANY to pay its EMPLOYEES and shall be conclusive as to the allowable, billable time to CLIENT for each such EMPLOYEE.

ARTICLE 4

WORKING HOURS

4.1 Work Week –

The work week for each EMPLOYEE shall begin at 12:01 A.M. Monday morning. A minimum of forty (40) hours of work shall be provided by CLIENT for each week for each EMPLOYEE assigned to CLIENT's work. This may be reduced to thirty-two (32) hours of work for any week wherein one of COMPANY's six (6) holidays is celebrated. When EMPLOYEE starts after Monday of EMPLOYEE's

NTSA DOCUMENT 771 • MEMBER-CLIENT AGREEMENT (COMPANY'S PREMISES) JULY 1971 EDITION
© 1971 NATIONAL TECHNICAL SERVICES ASSOCIATION • 1255 Twenty-Third Street, N.W. • Washington, D.C. 20037 • (202) 452-8100

first week, or is terminated prior to Friday of the final week, this condition shall not be applicable.

4.2 Overtime –

Overtime hours shall be defined as those hours worked in excess of eight (8) hours per day or forty (40) hours per week.

ARTICLE 5

COMPENSATION – EXPENSES

5.1 Hourly Billing Rates –

The fixed hourly billing rates listed below include the costs of maintaining proper payroll and accounting records, workmen's compensation insurance, federal and state unemployment insurance, social security, and other applicable payroll taxes, and also the labor rate, profit and all other overhead and administrative costs to be incurred by COMPANY:

Classification	S.T. Rate	O.T. Rate

5.2 Holidays and Vacations – Plant Closings –

The fixed hourly billing rates also include as an overhead item the labor cost of six (6) holidays observed by COMPANY and any paid vacation to which EMPLOYEE may be entitled under COMPANY's policies. The holidays observed by COMPANY are: New Year's Day, Memorial Day, Independence Day, Labor Day, Thanksgiving and Christmas.

5.2.1 All other plant closings of CLIENT during a work week in excess of the six (6) holidays listed above which prevent EMPLOYEES from working shall require payment of COMPANY's straight time billing rate for EMPLOYEES' services for any hours so lost. If work and any required liaison is provided by CLIENT, it may be possible for EMPLOYEES to continue work on such other plant closings.

5.2.2 COMPANY shall bill only straight time rates for the first eight (8) hours of work performed on a

COMPANY holiday which occurs on Monday through Friday.

5.2.3 COMPANY shall not bill for time lost by an EMPLOYEE because of illness or any other EMPLOYEE personal reason.

5.3 Travel on Client's Business –

In the event EMPLOYEES are required to travel on CLIENT's business, expenses incurred in such travel; i.e., air fare or other approved transportation, plus other expenses incidental for such travel, will be advanced to EMPLOYEE by COMPANY and billed to CLIENT at cost. Time worked for such EMPLOYEES shall be paid on the basis of the work week as outlined in 4.1 above, while on such assignments. EMPLOYEES traveling on CLIENT's business shall travel and work under the same rules, regulations and receive the same monetary reimbursements as CLIENT's employees of comparable responsibility. CLIENT shall authorize such travel in advance and shall advise EMPLOYEES and COMPANY of such rules, regulations and monetary reimbursement policies prior to EMPLOYEE's commencement of such travel.

5.4 Facilities, Materials and Supplies –

COMPANY shall provide all facilities, space and normal drafting equipment that may be required for EMPLOYEES to perform their assigned duties. COMPANY will provide desk space on its premises for one CLIENT representative for each twenty EMPLOYEES performing work for CLIENT. COMPANY shall provide roll vellum, consumable normal drafting supplies, and one check print of each finished drawing. All other materials, supplies, equipment and services required to perform work for CLIENT shall be billed to CLIENT at COMPANY's actual direct costs under paragraph 5.5.

5.5 Other Direct Expenses –

Subject to 5.4 above, COMPANY shall be reimbursed for actual direct expenses, which are *solely attributable* to the subject program, including but not limited to prints, sepias, security costs, models, telephone toll calls, telegrams and postage and any other direct expenses authorized in advance or ratified by the CLIENT.

5.6 Billing –

COMPANY will render invoices weekly for technical services performed under this contract. The terms of payment for this billing are

5.6.1 COMPANY will render invoices weekly for any other authorized out-of-pocket expenses. This billing will be payable in full upon receipt.

5.6.2 All invoices shall contain the following certification made by a duly authorized representative of COMPANY:

"I hereby certify that the above bill is correct and just and that payment therefor has not been received."

5

ARTICLE 6

INSURANCE

6.1 COMPANY will secure and maintain workmen's compensation and general liability insurance coverage to protect CLIENT from claims under Workmen's Compensation Acts and from claims for bodily injury, death or property damage, which may arise as a result of EMPLOYEES presence on CLIENT's premises. Upon request, certificates of insurance shall be submitted to CLIENT in conformance with COMPANY's standard coverages.

ARTICLE 7

TERMINATION

7.1 This agreement may be terminated at any time by either party upon ten (10) days notice in writing to the other party. In the event of termination, all CLIENT property and work in process in COMPANY's possession shall be forwarded to CLIENT and CLIENT shall make prompt payment for services performed to the effective date of termination.

ARTICLE 8

AMENDMENTS

8.1 This agreement may be amended from time to time by mutual agreement of the parties, executed and approved in the same manner as this agreement.

ARTICLE 9

INTERPRETATION

9.1 This agreement shall be construed and interpreted solely in accordance with the laws of the State of

ARTICLE 10

NOTICES

10.1 Whenever any notice is required or authorized to be given hereunder, such notice shall be given in writing and sent by registered mail. Any such notice, if sent by CLIENT to COMPANY, should be addressed as follows:

_____

_____

_____

If sent by COMPANY to CLIENT, any such notice should be addressed as follows:

_____

_____

_____

ARTICLE 11

ADDITIONAL TERMS AND CONDITIONS

NTSA DOCUMENT 771 • MEMBER-CLIENT AGREEMENT (COMPANY'S PREMISES) JULY 1971 EDITION
©1971 NATIONAL TECHNICAL SERVICES ASSOCIATION • 1255 Twenty-Third Street, N.W. • Washington, D.C. 20037 • (202) 452-8100

ARTICLE 11 (cont'd)

ADDITIONAL TERMS AND CONDITIONS

IN WITNESS WHEREOF, the parties hereto have made and executed this Agreement as of the day and year first above written.

CLIENT: COMPANY:

_____   _____

By _____   By _____

_____   _____

Title _____ Date _____   Title _____ Date _____

7

NTSA DOCUMENT 771 • MEMBER-CLIENT AGREEMENT (COMPANY'S PREMISES) JULY 1971 EDITION
© 1971 NATIONAL TECHNICAL SERVICES ASSOCIATION • 1255 Twenty-Third Street, N.W. • Washington, D.C. 20037 • (202) 452-8100

Appendix C

STANDARD FORM OF AGREEMENT

for

TECHNICAL SERVICES

on

TIME AND MATERIAL BASIS ON CLIENT'S PREMISES

AGREEMENT

BETWEEN

_____

AND

_____

RECOMMENDED BY THE NATIONAL TECHNICAL SERVICES ASSOCIATION

national technical
services association

NTSA DOCUMENT 470 • MEMBER-CLIENT AGREEMENT (CLIENTS' PREMISES) APRIL 1970 EDITION
© 1970 NATIONAL TECHNICAL SERVICES ASSOCIATION • 1255 Twenty-Third Street, N.W. • Washington, D.C. 20037 • (202) 452-8100

Reprinted by permission of the National Technical Services Association.

NTSA RECOMMENDED
STANDARD FORM OF AGREEMENT

For Technical Services
On Time And Material Basis On Client's Premises

TABLE OF CONTENTS

NTSA DOCUMENT 470 • MEMBER-CLIENT AGREEMENT (CLIENTS' PREMISES) APRIL 1970 EDITION
©1970 NATIONAL TECHNICAL SERVICES ASSOCIATION • 1255 Twenty-Third Street, N.W. • Washington, D.C. 20037 • (202) 452-8100

AGREEMENT

THIS AGREEMENT, made this _____ day of _____ 19_____ by and between

_____ (hereinafter called CLIENT)

and_____ (hereinafter called COMPANY).

WITNESSETH:

That, whereas the CLIENT desires technical services to be performed *on the CLIENT's premises* by employees of the COMPANY, and whereas the COMPANY agrees to provide such employees to perform such technical services.

NOW, THEREFORE, the CLIENT and the COMPANY in consideration of the mutual covenants hereinafter set forth and intending to be legally bound hereby AGREE as follows:

ARTICLE 1

COMPANY EMPLOYEES

1.1   Independent Contractor –

COMPANY is an independent contractor. The personnel assigned to CLIENT's premises by COMPANY are employees of COMPANY and are hereinafter called EMPLOYEE or EMPLOYEES. Such EMPLOYEES shall be paid for their services only by COMPANY. All matters concerning wages, expenses, hours worked and paid, working conditions, and other similar administrative matters shall be resolved between EMPLOYEE and COMPANY and not between EMPLOYEE and CLIENT.

1.2   Employment Terms – Confidentiality –

COMPANY shall inform its EMPLOYEES that the rate of pay and other emoluments and benefits of EMPLOYEE are a confidential matter between EMPLOYEE and COMPANY and are not to be disclosed to CLIENT's employees. Such a disclosure to CLIENT's employees may be grounds for immediate dismissal of EMPLOYEE.

1.3   Conformity With Client's Rules –

COMPANY will recognize all applicable rules, regulations or policies established by CLIENT on whose premises EMPLOYEE performs services. COMPANY shall inform EMPLOYEES that they are to abide by such regulations and policies and COMPANY shall further assist CLIENT in their implementation and enforcement.

1.4   Materials and Supplies –

CLIENT shall furnish all materials, supplies, facilities, space and equipment that may be required for EMPLOYEES to perform their assigned duties.

1.5   Satisfactory Performance –

If any EMPLOYEE assigned to CLIENT's work does not satisfactorily perform his assigned duties, or if CLIENT considers EMPLOYEE's conduct detrimental to CLIENT's overall program, COMPANY shall withdraw such EMPLOYEE immediately upon CLIENT's notification. CLIENT shall be responsible to pay COMPANY for the period of time EMPLOYEE was assigned to CLIENT.

1.6   Solicitation of Employees –

Neither CLIENT nor COMPANY shall solicit, approach or hire any of the other's employees for the purpose of employment by the other so long as this agreement is in effect and shall not have been terminated and for a period of ninety (90) days thereafter, except with the written consent of the other party.

1.7   Equal Employment Opportunity –

COMPANY and CLIENT agree to apply uniform and equitable standards of employment opportunity and assure that the best possible use is made of the abilities of EMPLOYEES regardless of race, creed, color, sex or age.

1.8   Employee Selection –

EMPLOYEES shall be selected by COMPANY in accordance with COMPANY's understanding of CLIENT's technical requirements. Because these requirements are subject to interpretation, final acceptance of EMPLOYEES remains the CLIENT's responsibility. After assignment, EMPLOYEES shall perform under the CLIENT's technical direction.

NTSA DOCUMENT 470 • MEMBER-CLIENT AGREEMENT (CLIENTS' PREMISES) APRIL 1970 EDITION
© 1970 NATIONAL TECHNICAL SERVICES ASSOCIATION • 1255 Twenty-Third Street, N.W. • Washington, D.C. 20037 • (202) 452-8100

ARTICLE 2

PROPRIETARY INFORMATION – INVENTIONS AND DISCOVERIES

2.1   Proprietary Information –

COMPANY informs its employees that private or proprietary information of its clients may become available to them. COMPANY instructs its employees to maintain such confidentiality and, where requested, requires that employees agree in writing substantially as follows:

2.1.1 All information (pertaining to COMPANY's or its clients' inventions, designs, tools, equipment, un-published written materials, plans, processes, costs, methods, systems, improvements, or other private or proprietary matters) which is obtained by employees in the performance of their work and which is not publicly disclosed by COMPANY or its clients shall be con-sidered as private and proprietary to COMPANY or to its clients whoever supplies or provides such informa-tion. Employees shall not, at any time during or after such employment, disclose such information nor the nature of the service which they render for COMPANY or its clients, except to authorized representatives of COMPANY or its clients.

The foregoing provisions in this paragraph shall be for the benefit of both COMPANY and its clients to whose work COMPANY's employees are assigned, and either COMPANY or its clients shall have all rights and remedies to enforce such provisions.

2.1.2 COMPANY will assign to clients, where re-quested, all of COMPANY's rights and remedies under the above provisions.

2.2   Inventions and Discoveries –

COMPANY requires each of its employees to execute an agreement which assigns to COMPANY, or its nominee, all and any discoveries and/or inventions as specified in paragraph 2.2.1 below. COMPANY will assign to clients, as its nominee, COMPANY's rights under these agreements.

2.2.1 The agreement states in part as follows:

All and any discoveries and/or inventions (which shall include improvements and modifications, but shall not be limited thereto) relating to work per-formed by employees, or relating to matters disclosed to employees in connection with work to be performed, or suggested by such matters, whether or not patent-able, which discoveries and/or inventions are made or conceived by employees, solely or jointly with others, during the term of their employment (regardless of whether conceived or developed during working hours), or during a period of one (1) year thereafter, shall be the property of COMPANY or its nominee and such dis-coveries and/or inventions shall be promptly disclosed to COMPANY.

COMPANY, or its nominee, shall have the right to file and prosecute, at its own expense, all patent applications; whether U.S. or foreign, on said discoveries and/or inventions. Employees shall, during their employment, at any time or times thereafter, provide to COMPANY or its nominee, all documents, information and assistance requested for the filing or prosecution of any such patent application, for the prep-aration, prosecution or defense of any legal action or application pertaining to such discoveries and/or in-ventions and for the assignment or conveyance to COM-PANY, or its nominee, of all right, title and interest in and to such discoveries and/or inventions, patent applica-tions and letters patent issuing thereon. Employees shall, in addition to the foregoing, upon request by COM-PANY, execute and deliver to COMPANY such agree-ments, pertaining to discoveries and/or inventions, as may at any time during the period of employees' em-ployment, be requested of COMPANY by clients, to whose work employee is assigned.

ARTICLE 3

RECORDS

3.1   Accounting Records –

COMPANY shall maintain complete and accurate accounting records in accordance with standard accounting practice to substantiate all charges hereunder. Such records may include payroll records, job cards, attendance records and summaries, and COMPANY shall retain such records for a period of three (3) years from date of final invoice.

3.2   Time Records –

COMPANY will provide each EMPLOYEE with weekly time tickets and/or time cards. Such time records shall be maintained by EMPLOYEE on a daily basis and, at the end of each week, the hours of work of each EM-PLOYEE assigned to CLIENT's work shall be approved by CLIENT and transmitted to COMPANY (by mutual agree-ment the CLIENT's time records system may be substituted for the COMPANY's system). These CLIENT approved time records will be used by the COMPANY to pay its EMPLOYEES and shall be conclusive as to the allowable, billable time to CLIENT for each such EMPLOYEE.

ARTICLE 4

WORKING HOURS

4.1   Work Week –

The work week for each EMPLOYEE shall begin at 12:01 A.M. Monday morning. A minimum of forty (40) hours of work shall be provided by CLIENT for each week for each EMPLOYEE assigned to CLIENT's facility. This may be reduced to thirty-two (32) hours of work for any week wherein one of COMPANY's six (6) holidays is

194 *Alternative Staffing Strategies*

celebrated. When EMPLOYEE starts after Monday of EMPLOYEE's first week, or is terminated prior to Friday of the final week, this condition shall not be applicable.

4.2 Overtime –
Overtime hours shall be defined as those hours worked in excess of eight (8) hours per day or forty (40) hours per week.

ARTICLE 5

COMPENSATION – EXPENSES

5.1 Hourly Billing Rates –
The fixed hourly billing rates listed below include the costs of maintaining proper payroll and accounting records, workmen's compensation insurance, federal and state unemployment insurance, social security, and other applicable payroll taxes, and also the labor rate, profit and all other overhead and administrative costs to be incurred by COMPANY:

Classification	S.T. Rate	O.T. Rate

5.2 Holidays and Vacations – Plant Closings –
The fixed hourly billing rates also include as an overhead item the labor cost of six (6) holidays observed by COMPANY and any paid vacation to which EMPLOYEE may be entitled under COMPANY's policies. The holidays observed by COMPANY are: New Year's Day, Memorial Day, Independence Day, Labor Day, Thanksgiving and Christmas.

5.2.1 All other plant closings of CLIENT during a work week in excess of the six (6) holidays listed above which prevent EMPLOYEES from working shall require payment of COMPANY's straight time billing rate for EMPLOYEES' services for any hours so lost.

5.2.2 COMPANY shall bill only straight time rates for the first eight (8) hours of work performed on a COMPANY holiday which occurs on Monday through Friday.

5.2.3 COMPANY shall not bill for time lost by an EMPLOYEE because of illness or any other EMPLOYEE personal reason.

5.3 Living Expense Allowance –
The living expense allowance for each EMPLOYEE is based on living expenses for an entire day, shall be $ _____ per day, seven (7) days per week, and, during EMPLOYEE's eligibility for such payment, is to be paid for each day, commencing with the day EMPLOYEE reports for work and ending on EMPLOYEE's last day of work at CLIENT's facility, without consideration of hours worked or reduction for absence due to sickness or injury or holiday.

5.4 Travel Expense To and From Assignment –
When an EMPLOYEE is assigned to a CLIENT's premises which is outside the local area of the point of origin of EMPLOYEE, the COMPANY will be reimbursed for EMPLOYEE's actual reporting travel expenses to CLIENT's premises in an amount not to exceed the equivalent of one-way tourist air fare (or equivalent mileage at ten cents per mile) from any point of origin within the continental United States (excepting the states of Alaska and Hawaii) to the CLIENT's premises. An equal reimbursement will be made for such travel expenses incurred for the EMPLOYEE's return to his point of origin at the termination of the assignment.

5.5 Travel on Client's Business –
In the event EMPLOYEES are required to travel on CLIENT's business, expenses incurred in such travel; i.e., air fare or other approved transportation, plus other expenses incidental for such travel, will be advanced to EMPLOYEE by COMPANY and billed to CLIENT at cost. Time worked for such EMPLOYEES shall be paid on the basis of the work week as outlined in 4.1 above, while on such assignments. EMPLOYEES traveling on CLIENT's business shall travel and work under the same rules, regulations and receive the same monetary reimbursements as CLIENT's employees of comparable responsibility. CLIENT shall authorize such travel in advance and shall advise EMPLOYEES and COMPANY of such rules, regulations and monetary reimbursement policies prior to EMPLOYEE's commencement of such travel.

5.6 Other Direct Expenses –
COMPANY shall be reimbursed for actual direct expenses, which are *solely attributable* to the subject program, including but not limited to prints, sepias, security costs, models, telephone toll calls, telegrams, postage and any other direct expenses authorized in advance or ratified by the CLIENT.

5.7 Billing –
COMPANY will render invoices weekly for technical services performed under this contract. The terms of payment for this billing are _____

5.7.1 COMPANY will render invoices weekly for any other authorized out-of-pocket expenses. This billing will be payable in full upon receipt.

NTSA DOCUMENT 470 • MEMBER-CLIENT AGREEMENT (CLIENTS' PREMISES) APRIL 1970 EDITION
©1970 NATIONAL TECHNICAL SERVICES ASSOCIATION • 1255 Twenty-Third Street, N.W. • Washington, D.C. 20037 • (202) 452-8100

5.72. All invoices shall contain the following certification made by a duly authorized representative of COMPANY:

> "I hereby certify that the above bill is correct and just and that payment therefor has not been received."

ARTICLE 6

INSURANCE

6.1 COMPANY will secure and maintain workmen's compensation and general liability insurance coverage to protect CLIENT from claims under Workmen's Compensation Acts and from claims for bodily injury, death or property damage, which may arise as a result of EMPLOYEES presence on CLIENT's premises. Upon request, certificates of insurance shall be submitted to CLIENT in conformance with COMPANY's standard coverages.

ARTICLE 7

TERMINATION

7.1 This agreement may be terminated at any time by either party upon ten (10) days notice in writing to the other party. In the event of termination, all CLIENT property and work in process in COMPANY's possession shall be forwarded to CLIENT and CLIENT shall make prompt payment for services performed to the effective date of termination.

ARTICLE 8

AMENDMENTS

8.1 This agreement may be amended from time to time by mutual agreement of the parties, executed and approved in the same manner as this agreement.

ARTICLE 9

INTERPRETATION

9.1 This agreement shall be construed and interpreted solely in accordance with the laws of the State of

_____ .

ARTICLE 10

NOTICES

10.1 Whenever any notice is required or authorized to be given hereunder, such notice shall be given in writing and sent by registered mail. Any such notice, if sent by CLIENT to COMPANY, should be addressed as follows:

_____

_____

_____

If sent by COMPANY to CLIENT, any such notice should be addressed as follows:

_____

_____

_____

ARTICLE 11

ADDITIONAL TERMS AND CONDITIONS

NTSA DOCUMENT 470 • MEMBER-CLIENT AGREEMENT (CLIENTS' PREMISES) APRIL 1970 EDITION
© 1970 NATIONAL TECHNICAL SERVICES ASSOCIATION • 1255 Twenty-Third Street, N.W. • Washington, D.C. 20037 • (202) 452-8100

6

ARTICLE 11 (cont'd)

ADDITIONAL TERMS AND CONDITIONS

IN WITNESS WHEREOF, the parties hereto have made and executed this Agreement as of the day and year first above written.

CLIENT: COMPANY:

_____   _____

By _____   By _____

_____   _____

Title _____ Date _____   Title _____ Date _____

NTSA DOCUMENT 470 • MEMBER-CLIENT AGREEMENT (CLIENTS' PREMISES) APRIL 1970 EDITION
©1970 NATIONAL TECHNICAL SERVICES ASSOCIATION • 1255 Twenty-Third Street, N.W. • Washington, D.C. 20037 • (202) 452-8100

Index

About the Author

David Nye is currently Assistant Professor of Management at Athens State College, Athens, Alabama. He previously taught management, personnel, and small business courses at the University of Maryland-University College at College Park, Maryland, and at the George Washington University Center for Continuing Education in Washington, D.C. During his career in industry, he was corporate Manager, Personnel Administration, for The Standard Oil Company, and earlier held management positions in personnel and human resources at ICI Americas Inc. and Joy Manufacturing Company.

He received an MBA from Virginia Commonwealth University in 1977.

Author of numerous articles on employment issues, Professor Nye has contributed to such publications as the *AMA Management Digest*, *Harvard Business Review*, *National Business Employment Weekly*, and *Across the Board*.